Cognitive Behaviour Therapy

SECOND EDITION

Your route out of perfectionism, self-sabotage and other everyday habits with CBT

AVY JOSEPH

CAPSTONE
A Wiley Brand

This updated edition first published 2016

© 2016 Avy Joseph

First edition published 2009

Registered office

John Wiley and Sons Ltd, The Atrium, Southern Gate, Chichester, West Sussex, PO19 8SQ, United Kingdom

For details of our global editorial offices, for customer services and for information about how to apply for permission to reuse the copyright material in this book please see our website at www.wiley.com.

Wiley publishes in a variety of print and electronic formats and by print-on-demand. Some material included with standard print versions of this book may not be included in e-books or in print-on-demand. If this book refers to media such as a CD or DVD that is not included in the version you purchased, you may download this material at http://booksupport.wiley.com. For more information about Wiley products, visit www.wiley.com.

Designations used by companies to distinguish their products are often claimed as trademarks. All brand names and product names used in this book and on its cover are trade names, service marks, trademark or registered trademarks of their respective owners. The publisher and the book are not associated with any product or vendor mentioned in this book. None of the companies referenced within the book have endorsed the book.

Library of Congress Cataloging-in-Publication Data

Names: Joseph, Avy, author.
Title: Cognitive behaviour therapy : your route out of perfectionism, self-sabotage and other everyday habits with CBT / Avy Joseph.
Description: Second edition. | Chichester, West Sussex : John Wiley & Sons, Inc., [2016] Includes index.
Identifiers: LCCN 2015041919 (print) | LCCN 2015042202 (ebook) |
  ISBN 9780857086471 (paperback) | ISBN 9780857086488 (pdf) |
  ISBN 9780857086495 (epub)
Subjects: LCSH: Cognitive therapy—Popular works. | BISAC: PSYCHOLOGY / Psychotherapy / General.
Classification: LCC RC489.C63 J67 2016 (print) | LCC RC489.C63 (ebook) |
  DDC 616.89/1425—dc23
LC record available at http://lccn.loc.gov/2015041919

Cover design: Wiley

Set in 11/14pt and Sabon LT Std by SPi-Global, Chennai, India
Printed in Great Britain by TJ International Ltd, Padstow, Cornwall, UK

I wish to dedicate this book to the memory of my father who passed away nine years ago.

Contents

Acknowledgements

Chris Hynes for unconditional love, help and support. My family for the love and encouragement.

Professor Windy Dryden for his clinical and professional guidance. Maggie Chapman for her friendship and professional support.

Introduction to the Second Edition

Cognitive Behaviour Therapy (CBT) is recognized as one of the leading, evidence-based talking therapies. CBT places much emphasis on currently held beliefs and attitudes, painful emotions, and problematic behaviours that can sabotage a fuller experience of life. CBT teaches us a philosophy of life that can be learned by everyone in order to be happier.

The ideas and philosophies in CBT stem from ancient and modern philosophers, science, psychology, common sense and humanity. CBT is supported by a wealth of research, is used extensively by the NHS and is recommended by NICE (National Institute for Health and Clinical Excellence) for many emotional and psychological problems.

There are many types of CBT. Rational Emotive Behaviour Therapy (REBT) is one of the cognitive behaviour therapies under the CBT umbrella. It is an evidence-based, psycho-educational and philosophical model developed by Albert Ellis. Since the first edition, REBT has continued to grow. Research in REBT has demonstrated both its effectiveness and efficacy for both clinical and non-clinical problems.

REBT is grounded in acceptance: acceptance of the past, present, future and of the self, other and life. Acceptance does not mean approval. Sometimes people ask 'but if I accept failure then doesn't it mean that I'm okay with it or that I didn't mind failing?' The answer is an absolute no. Failure does matter to most people, and most of us don't like it, but it does happen. Acceptance means acknowledgement of this reality, in this particular example. When we overcome this misunderstanding, self-confidence, emotional health and well-being and life goals become much easier to achieve.

This second edition is more concise than the first with more practical applications and tips. Some concepts are repeated in different ways. This is deliberate. Repetition helps us internalize the learning in order for it to become habitual and effortless.

The ideas in this book are heavily influenced by REBT theory but some concepts stem from other CBT models and self-image psychology. In this book I will show you how using CBT can help you set yourself up for success and overcome those beliefs and habits that sabotage your life.

Avy Joseph

1
Understanding CBT for Goal Achievement

'People are not disturbed by events but by the
view they hold about them.'

Epictetus, Stoic philosopher c. AD 75

This chapter will introduce you to some of the basic ideas and principles of Cognitive Behaviour Therapy (CBT) and how you can use it to help you achieve your goals. First though, what does Cognitive Behaviour Therapy (CBT) actually mean?

Cognitive simply means our 'thinking processes': how we think, how we acquire information and knowledge, how we store it in our head, how we evaluate it and how we base some of our decisions on it.

Behaviour means our action or reaction to something. It's the doing bit. Our behaviour can be conscious or unconscious (out of our conscious awareness). In CBT, the word 'behaviour' comes from a branch of psychology called 'behaviourism', which is concerned with what can be observed rather than what can be speculated or assumed. It is based on what you have learned and become accustomed to, how this affects your actions and feelings, and how you can unlearn what you have learned in order to change.

Therapy means the treatment for a health problem after a diagnosis or an assessment has been made.

CBT is a form of therapy that examines how our thinking, attitudes, beliefs, opinions and behaviour are formed, how they affect our success, our lives and feelings, and how changing them impacts on our performance. The ideas stem from both ancient and modern thinking in philosophy, science, psychology, common sense and humanity.

Here are some of basic principles central to CBT. Many may be shared by other therapeutic approaches, but the combination of these principles goes some way towards understanding CBT.

THE EMOTIONAL RESPONSIBILITY PRINCIPLE

'People are not disturbed by events but by the view they hold about them.'

This principle is at the heart of nearly all emotional and behavioural change. It can be challenging because you may believe that it's what has happened to you that 'makes' you feel how you feel and do what you do in the here and now.

I hope that by questioning this you will learn that what you believe may be stopping you from empowering yourself to move forward with your life. This in turn may help you in the pursuit of your desired goals.

Is it true that events, situations or people make us feel what we feel?

First, let's look at the popular notion that your feelings are 'caused' by events, situations or other people.

Think of a past event that you think 'made' you feel and do something. By this logic the only way you can change your feelings now is to wish the event had not happened in the first place.

Maybe you think there's someone else who has 'made' you feel and act in a certain manner. In which case, the only way you can change your feelings now is to get that person from the past to undo what they did or said. And if that person is now deceased, how can this be done?

Believing that the past, or a particular situation or person, causes our feelings today, means that no one would ever be able to move forward or to change. We would all be totally stuck without any possibility or hope of ever changing anything. We would be slaves to the things that had happened to us or the people we had been involved with.

Can you imagine what it would be like if everyone felt hurt every time they experienced a rejection of some sort?

Rejection = Hurt

10 people rejected = 10 people feeling hurt

100 people rejected = 100 people feeling hurt

1000 people rejected = 1000 people feeling hurt

As an example, when you experience rejection you *might* feel hurt. However, if you believe that your feelings are caused by others, you may then believe that being rejected by someone is the cause of your hurt feelings. But don't some of us experience different emotions if rejected by someone we like? Maybe anger, sadness, depression or relief?

In fact, different people may feel different emotions when they experience the same event:

Some people feel hurt
Some people feel angry
Some people feel depressed
Some people couldn't care less

Why do different people feel different things and what is at the heart of their feelings?

Is it true that events or people make us do what we do?

Let's think about what we do and assume that situations or people make us behave as we do.

A colleague criticizes you = You start avoiding them

If it is true that a colleague's criticism 'made' you avoid them, this means that every criticism made by your colleague would have the same effect on everyone. It means that avoidance is the only possibility whenever your colleague criticizes you, or anyone else for that matter.

A colleague criticizes 10 people = 10 people avoid them

A colleague criticizes 100 people = 100 people avoid them

A colleague criticizes 1000 people = 1000 people avoid them

Does this make sense?

The problem is that people say, 'he made me do it' or 'she made me lose my temper'. It is as if they have absolutely no control over their behaviour. Once again, if we do not have a part to play in how we behave then we would be completely stuck, unable to move forward, learn or do anything useful. Is this what you see happening to everyone around you?

So what provokes your feelings and behaviour? Most of the time the simple answer is that you do. You provoke your feelings and actions by the way you think, the attitudes you've formed, the habits you no longer question and the beliefs you hold.

This is the principle of emotional responsibility: **you are largely responsible for the way you feel and act.**

The principle of emotional responsibility can be challenging, particularly if you are going through a difficult time or have experienced trauma or personal tragedy. It's natural to feel angry, sad, depressed or hurt in response to accidents, illness and other challenges in life, but if you get stuck in these feelings then you can change them.

> The thought manifests as the word; The word manifests as the deed; The deed develops into habit;
>
> And habit hardens into character;
>
> So watch the thought and its ways with care. (Buddha)

The way you think about something affects how you feel and how you behave. Here are some examples:

- If you think that your partner's late arrival for dinner proves that you are not lovable then you might feel hurt and sulk.
- If you think that your partner was nasty and selfish because they arrived late for dinner then you might feel angry and shout.
- If you think that your partner's late arrival for dinner is no big deal then you can feel calm about it and ask what happened.

This shows that it is not the situation or what happens to us that provokes our feelings and behaviour. It is the way we think about the situation. The way we think about something can then influence how we behave.

THE BEHAVIOURAL PRINCIPLE

CBT considers behaviour as significant in maintaining or in changing psychological states. If, for example, you avoid some event, such as giving a presentation to your team, then you will deny yourself the opportunity to disconfirm your negative thoughts about yourself or capabilities. Furthermore, avoidance only sabotages what you want to achieve. Changing what you do is often a powerful way of helping you change thoughts and emotions and ultimately what you can achieve.

THE 'HERE AND NOW' PRINCIPLE

Traditional therapies take the view that looking at problems in the here and now is superficial. They consider successful treatment must uncover the childhood developmental issues, hidden motivations and unconscious conflicts that are supposed to lie at the root of the problem. These approaches argue that treating the current problem rather than the supposed hidden 'root' causes would result in symptom substitution, that is the problem would re-surface in another form later on. There is little evidence to support this idea. Behaviour therapy also showed that such an outcome, although possible, was very rare.

CBT offers theories about how current problems are being maintained and kept alive and how they can be changed.

THE SCIENTIFIC PRINCIPLE

CBT offers scientific theories. Scientific theories are designed in a way so they can be tested. CBT has been evaluated rigorously using evidence rather than just clinical anecdote. This is important for a couple of reasons:

- The treatment can be founded on sound and well-established theories.
- Ethically, CBT therapists can have confidence in the therapy they are advocating.

Exercise

List five things that people manage to change about themselves despite doing it badly at first (for example, learning to drive).

1.
2.

3.
4.
5.

List five positive things that you have learned in your life despite experiencing difficulties (for example, moving on from a failed relationship).

1.
2.
3.
4.
5.

Think of an inspirational person who has overcome enormous obstacles by having a powerful and constructive attitude and positive behaviour.

Truth

In CBT we examine our thoughts and behaviours to check if they are realistic. This means we judge and evaluate an event based on facts rather than perception, which can be flawed. Why do you think that, when an accident occurs, the police take statements from a number of people instead of asking just one person what happened?

Truth is about being consistent with reality whilst striving for the goals that are important to you. It's about acknowledging and accepting the existence of the possibilities you dislike while persisting in your efforts to reach your goals.

Exercise

How many 'F's can you count in the following statement?

FINISHED FILES ARE THE RESULTS OF YEARS OF SCIENTIFIC STUDY COMBINED WITH THE EXPERIENCE OF MANY YEARS.

Did you see 2 or 3 'F's?

There are 6.

I will leave you to find the rest but simply draw your attention to the word 'of.'

The above is a popular example used to highlight the fact that we don't necessarily see the whole truth. We interpret what we see and experience. What you have learnt from this simple but effective exercise is that your version of the truth can be faulty. It is important to question the truth that you hold about yourself and your ability just in case you are seeing only a few of the good things and missing many others. Sometimes we only see a few 'F's, when in reality there are more. If the 'F's represent your positive abilities and qualities, how many of the good qualities are you seeing?

This is just one of the reasons why in CBT we question the validity or reality of our thoughts.

Common sense

In CBT we suggest taking a logical and common-sense approach to thinking.

This does not mean that you become totally unfeeling and emotionless.

Logic or common sense is about the purity of our reasoning skills, whether a conclusion correctly follows a premise or assumption.

For example, which one of these two statements makes sense?

> A. Some men shave their heads . . . therefore anyone with a shaved head is a man.

> B. Some men shave their heads . . . but it doesn't mean everyone with a shaved head is a man.

Clearly statement B makes sense. In statement A, the fact that some men shave their heads does not connect logically to the assumption that anyone with a shaved head is a man. Some women, children and teenagers also have shaved heads.

Logical thinking is useful because we all have the ability to think and use common sense. In CBT, using your common sense well can lead you to form better conclusions about yourself.

Some people think like this about certain goals:

I failed at achieving my goal	*therefore, I am a total failure as a person*

Others think like this:

I failed at achieving my goal	*but that doesn't mean I am a total failure. I am fallible but worthwhile nevertheless. I will learn from my failure and improve.*

Which of the above two statements makes sense?

Helpfulness

Finally, in CBT we look at how helpful your thoughts are to you and in the pursuit of your goals. Your thoughts are responsible for how you feel about yourself and your abilities, so it is more helpful for you to have constructive and goal-oriented thoughts than not.

Exercise

Reflect on some thoughts you often have about yourself and your abilities. See if they are helpful to you. For example, you might think 'I'm not very good at talking in front of people.'

How can you make your thoughts more realistic, logical and helpful? For example, 'I could improve by facing my fears slowly and gradually.'

TYPES OF THOUGHTS

In CBT we draw a distinction between different types of thoughts. Not all of our thoughts are involved with our feelings and behaviours. The thoughts that are involved in our feelings tend to have some sort of an assumption or judgement about ourselves, others or the world.

There are two particular types of thought that are involved in our emotions or feelings.

1. Inferences

Inferences are assumptions you make about the things that matter to you, which can be about yourself, others or about the world. For example, if your boss contradicted you during a meeting that was important to you, you might think, 'he is undermining me'. Then you would be making an inference. This means that in that moment you have gone beyond the facts and made an assumption about what happened because it was significant to you. In this example you would have an emotional response: you might feel annoyed, concerned, anxious, angry or some other negative emotion.

The issue is whether your boss was undermining you or simply expressing a different opinion. In order to find out you would need to gather more information and evidence. Some of our inferences are accurate and some are not. In this example your inference has not been tested in reality.

If you had thought 'he has a different opinion, he is not undermining me' then your emotional response would be different.

Which of the following thoughts will lead to an emotion?

1. *I saw a woman getting on a bus.*
2. *My workmates are ignoring me.*
3. *I'm a failure.*

Thoughts 2 and 3 will lead to an emotional reaction. The second thought is an inference. It may or may not be true. Your colleagues have been ignoring you – they may just have been very busy with work. You need more information to assess the accuracy of conclusion. But if you conclude that you were being ignored then you would have an emotional reaction.

The third thought also leads to an emotional response but it is more profound in its conclusion. 'I'm a failure' is an evaluative thought.

2. Evaluations or beliefs

Inferences influence our emotions but do not fully provoke them. Evaluations, on the other hand, are thoughts that are fully involved in provoking emotions and feelings. When you have an evaluative thought you are making a judgement about yourself, about others, or about the world. For simplicity let's call evaluative thoughts 'beliefs'. These are fundamental in provoking either constructive feelings and helpful behaviours or destructive feelings and sabotaging behaviours.

If you judge yourself as 'useless' when you are thinking about applying for a job, this may trigger additional thoughts such as 'I won't get the job'. When you hold such a belief, you will probably feel anxious when you go for the interview. In a state of anxiety, you will probably not perform as well as you are capable of doing and the likelihood of you getting the job decreases dramatically.

THEORY MADE SIMPLE

Putting these principles and philosophies into a theoretical model helps you to see more easily how feelings, different thoughts, behaviours and events all interact with one another.

The easiest is the 'ABC' model of emotional response.

A = Activating Event (or trigger)
B = Belief
C = Consequences

The 'A' can be:

1. **Real or imaginary**
   The trigger can be an actual event, such as losing someone or something important to you, or an imaginary one. It could also be an inference – a hunch – like imagining that someone is going to reject you before any rejection has taken place.
2. **External or internal**
   External events are things that happen outside of your body, for example: someone's death, being rejected, failing at something or experiencing an accident.
   Internal events are triggers that happen inside your body, for example: your thoughts, images, emotions, fantasies, memories and bodily sensations.

3. About the past, present or future

The event could be something that has happened in the past, something that is happening now or something that could happen in the future.

Key points to remember:

- 'A' can be an internal past event that was real. For example, losing someone you loved. All past events are internal because they exist in our memories.
- 'A' can be real, future and external. For example, making a speech at your friend's wedding next week.
- It is not the event itself that provokes your emotions but what you tell yourself or what you infer about it *now* that provokes your feeling.
- It's easy to assume that A causes C but that would not be accurate.

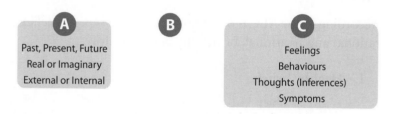

When the trigger happens at 'A', you feel, behave, think and experience symptoms. Because this happens quickly, you think 'A' causes 'C' (the consequences). So you may use expressions like 'he *made* me feel angry', or 'my job *makes* me depressed'. It is as if we are not responsible for our own emotions.

Remember the 100 and 1000 people example earlier?

What is at the heart of your feelings is the 'B' (Belief) between 'A' and 'C'. So it is your belief (evaluation) about the activating event that provokes your emotions, behaviours, thoughts and symptoms.

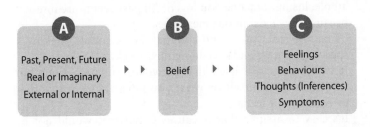

Beliefs

According to the ABC model we can have two types of beliefs: rational and irrational, or healthy and unhealthy.

1. **Healthy beliefs:**
   - are flexible;
   - are based on the things that you want, like, desire and prefer;
   - tend to make sense – they are logical and consistent with reality;
   - mean accepting that sometimes you may not get what you want;
   - detach human worth from success or failure;
   - lead to emotional well-being and set you up for goal achievement.

2. **Unhealthy beliefs:**
   - are unrealistic;
   - can be self-critical;

- are not based on acceptance or acknowledgement of reality;
- do not acknowledge or accept other possibilities (even though reality shows that other possibilities exist);
- cause a mismatch between internal and external realities;
- lead to emotional disturbance and set you up for failure and goal sabotage.

Compare the following statements:

'I would like it to be nice and sunny every day when I wake up but I accept there is a chance that it might not be.'

'The day MUST be nice and sunny when I wake up.'

The second example is unhealthy and irrational because it is unrealistic. Unhealthy beliefs do not make logical sense. What makes sense is to have a more healthy belief like: 'I would like the day to be nice and sunny when I wake up, but it doesn't mean that it HAS to be.'

Healthy negative emotions and self-helping behaviours

It is easy to understand that if you hold a healthy belief about yourself or about certain things in your life, this will increase your chances of success. However, success is never guaranteed, so if you don't succeed you might feel upset and sad. Having healthy beliefs means that, while you might feel sad or upset if you failed, you would lick your wounds, dust yourself off and focus back on your goal. Instead of feeling guilty you might feel regret and look at ways of improving. Instead of feeling unhealthy anger or rage, you might feel annoyed. You would behave assertively without lashing out in a destructive way or giving up. You would believe that you are not a failure as a human being but rather that you are a fallible human being who is able to learn and improve.

Unhealthy negative emotions and self-destructive behaviours

It is not difficult to understand that if you have unhealthy beliefs about yourself and about certain things in your life, your feelings and behaviours are not going to be healthy.

According to the ABC model, unhealthy beliefs provoke unhealthy, negative emotions and self-damaging or destructive behaviours. Depression, anxiety, guilt and rage are examples of unhealthy negative emotions.

ANXIETY VS CONCERN

Unhealthy negative emotion	What the belief is about	Healthy negative emotion
Anxiety	A threat or danger	Concern

How you think		**How you think**
You exaggerate the overall effect of the threat		You keep the effect of the danger in perspective
You think that you won't be able to deal with the danger		You have a balanced view about your ability to deal with the threat
You see the glass as half empty		You see the whole glass and focus on the full part
Your thoughts are not constructive		Your thoughts are solution-focused and constructive
What you do or want to do		**What you do or want to do**
Run away physically		Face the threat
Run away mentally		Deal with the potential danger
Do superstitious things to get rid of the threat		
Medicate and numb your feelings e.g. with alcohol		
Seek assurances from others		

DEPRESSION VS SADNESS

Unhealthy negative emotion	What the belief is about	Healthy negative emotion
Depression	Loss or failure	Sadness

How you think

You only focus on negatives since the loss or failure

You think of all the other past losses and failures

You think you are a failure, helpless

You think the future is hopeless, bleak and full of misery

What you do or want to do

You pull away from other people

You withdraw into your head

You stop looking after yourself and your environment

You get rid of your emotions in destructive ways, e.g. alcohol or overeating

How you think

You think of both the negatives and positives of the loss or failure

You do not dwell on past losses and failures

You do not see yourself as a failure or as helpless. You think that you can help yourself to move forward

You have hope for the future

What you do or want to do

You express how you feel about your loss or failure

You look after yourself and your environment

You engage in healthy behaviours

ANGER/RAGE VS ANNOYANCE

Unhealthy negative emotion	What the belief is about	Healthy negative emotion
Anger or rage	Loss or failure	Sadness

How you think	How you think
You exaggerate the actions of the person who has broken your personal rule	You are balanced about the intention behind the thing that was done
You think the other person's intentions were malicious	You don't see malice
You are right and the other person is definitely wrong	You are open to being wrong
You can't see the other person's point of view	You can listen to the other person's point of view
You think of how you can get your revenge	You do not think of seeking revenge
What you do or want to do	**What you do or want to do**
You physically attack	You talk and behave in an assertive manner but with the right intent
You verbally attack	
You pay them back somehow e.g. by ignoring them or staying silent	You ask the other person to make changes but you don't demand it
You recruit allies against the other person	

HURT VS SORROW

Unhealthy negative emotion	What the belief is about	Healthy negative emotion
Hurt	Someone has treated you badly. You think you deserve to be treated better	Sorrow

How you think

You exaggerate the unfairness of your treatment

You think the other person does not care about you

You think of yourself as unlovable or misunderstood

You remember the other times when you felt hurt

The other person must understand and make amends first

What you do or want to do

You sulk and shut down

You pick on the other person without telling them why

How you think

You think in a balanced way about the unfairness

You do not think the other person does not care about you

You do not think of yourself as unlovable or misunderstood

You don't think about the other times when you felt hurt

You don't insist the other person has to make the first move

What you do or want to do

You talk about how you feel in order to persuade the other person to behave more fairly

GUILT VS REMORSE

Unhealthy negative emotion	What the belief is about	Healthy negative emotion
Guilt	You have broken a moral code or the feelings of a significant person were hurt	Remorse

How you think

You have definitely committed a sin

You think you are more responsible than another

You forget about how things were

You deserve punishment

What you do or want to do

You escape from your feeling in destructive ways

You plead for forgiveness and/or punish yourself by physical deprivation

How you think

You think about what you did and put it in context before you make a judgement

You are balanced about your responsibility and the other person's

You acknowledged the situation and the circumstances before you did what you did

You don't think about retribution

What you do or want to do

You face up to the healthy pain

You ask for forgiveness but you do not physically punish yourself

You make unrealistic promises never to do it again You deny that you did anything bad	You make appropriate amends You accept your poor behaviour without making excuses

SHAME VS REGRET

Unhealthy negative emotion	What the belief is about	Healthy negative emotion
Shame or embarrassment	Something shameful has been revealed about you. Other people judge you or shun you	Regret

How you think

You exaggerate the shameful information revealed

You exaggerate the likelihood of negative judgement

You think the negative judgement will last a long time

You exaggerate the degree of negative judgement

How you think

You remain compassionate about yourself. You accept yourself

You are realistic about the likelihood of negative judgement

You are realistic about the length of negative judgement

You are realistic about the degree of negative judgement

What you do or want to do

You avoid eye contact with others

You avoid others

What you do or want to do

You continue participating in social events

You accept others' intervention to restore social harmony

You attack others who
    have shamed you
You defend your ego
    in self-defeating
    ways
You ignore others
    who attempt
    to help restore
    balance

UNHEALTHY ENVY VS HEALTHY ENVY

Unhealthy negative emotion	What the belief is about	Healthy negative emotion
Unhealthy envy	Another person has something you find desirable	Healthy envy

How you think

You devalue the desired object

You tell yourself that you don't want it, even if you do

You try to attain it, even if it is not useful to you

You put other people down and attempt to deprive them of the desired object

What you do or want to do

You belittle the desired object verbally

You belittle the other person verbally

You attempt to remove or deprive the other person from desired possession

You spoil or destroy the desired object or possession

How you think

You admit to yourself that you too desire it

You admit that you'd also want it and accept that you do

You find ways to attain it only because you want it

You do not put other people down and you allow them to enjoy it

What you do or want to do

You do not belittle the desired possession

You attempt to attain it but only if you want it

UNHEALTHY JEALOUSY VS HEALTHY JEALOUSY

Unhealthy negative emotion	What the belief is about	Healthy negative emotion
Unhealthy jealousy	There is a potential threat to a relationship from another person	Healthy jealousy

How you think

You see a threat to your relationship when none exists

You think infidelity will definitely happen

You misinterpret your partner's conversation with and actions towards another as having sexual or romantic meaning

What you do or want to do

You have visual images of infidelity

How you think

You do not see a threat where none exists

You do not think infidelity will definitely happen

You do not misinterpret your partner's conversation with and actions toward another as having sexual or romantic meaning

What you do or want to do

You do not have sexual images of your partner with another

If your partner admits to finding someone attractive, you see yourself as less attractive	You accept that your partner can find another attractive without thinking that you are less attractive
You want your partner to only ever think of you	You accept that your partner can see others as attractive just as you can

---

Exercise

Identify the different emotions in the example below and work out if they are healthy or unhealthy.

Sam is a 40-year-old man and has been married for three years. He is studying towards some professional qualifications and has to sit his final exams in a couple of months. He is finding it difficult to concentrate when he sits down to revise. He keeps thinking that he will fail and, whenever he tries to revise, he ends up doing other work. When his wife tells him to sit down and get on with it he slams his books shut and shouts at her. After his outburst he ends up begging for forgiveness and thinks that he is a bad person.

Answer at end of chapter

The following diagram illustrates key points in this chapter.

Cognitive Behaviour Therapy

Past, Present, Future   Real or Imaginary   External or Internal

B

Belief

Healthy or Rational | **Unhealthy or Irrational**

Well-being and Goal Achievement | **Disturbance and Goal Sabotage**

Healthy or Rational	Unhealthy or Irrational
Flexible: based on what you want/desire	Rigid: based on must/have to
Consistent with reality (I want but I accept that sometimes I might not get)	Inconsistent with reality (no allowance for other possibilities)
Makes sense (I want but it doesn't follow that I must have)	Doesn't make sense (I want and it follows that I must have)
Self/Other/World accepting	Self/Other/World damning
Healthy negative emotions and self-helping behaviours	Unhealthy negative emotions and goal sabotaging behaviours

Concern	Anxiety
Sadness	Depression
Annoyance	Anger
Remorse	Guilt
Healthy Envy	Unhealthy Envy
Regret	Shame/Embarrassment
Healthy Jealousy	Unhealthy Jealousy
Disappointment	Hurt

C

Feelings   Behaviours   Thoughts (Inferences)   Symptoms

---

*Answer to identifying emotions exercise: Anxiety – unhealthy negative emotion; Anger – unhealthy negative emotion; Guilt – unhealthy negative emotion.

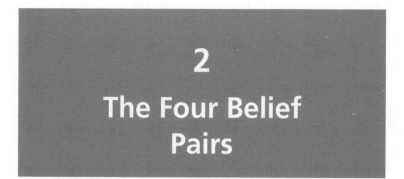

2
The Four Belief Pairs

In this chapter, you will learn about healthy and unhealthy beliefs in more detail. Understanding the following concepts will help you to identify what specifically makes beliefs and thoughts healthy or unhealthy.

WANT TO VS HAVE TO

Most of us talk about what we 'want to' do and what we 'must do' without paying too much attention to the meaning behind these expressions and the feelings they provoke. I want you to consider all the things that you feel are an absolute 'have to' in your life.

- Is it that you feel you 'have to' work?
- Could it be that you feel you 'have to' have love in your life?
- Maybe it's that you consider you 'have to' look after someone?
- Perhaps it's that you think you 'have to' achieve your dreams?

According to CBT, people have a tendency to take the things they want and desire and turn them into demands. For example, a child learns to play the piano because she really enjoys playing and loves the sound. She begins to practise harder and rapidly improves. She gets praised and this in turn motivates her to do more. She then has the opportunity to perform in front of her friends at school and she knows that everyone will be there watching her. She really wants to do well and not make a mistake when she is playing in front of all those people. She begins to think, 'I'm going to practise harder to ensure that I don't make a mistake'. Her friends ask her 'How are you feeling about playing? Aren't you scared about making a mistake?' A teacher may say, 'I hope you're practising because you don't want to make a mistake' and so on. She then begins to put pressure on herself by thinking, 'I must make sure that I don't make a mistake'. By the time of the performance she is in a state of fear because she is now telling herself that she 'has to' get it right.

This simple example illustrates how you can turn your 'want to' into a stressful 'have to'. This is simply a human trait – we all have the ability to turn our desires and wants into dogmatic and absolute 'have to's. Other words for 'have to' are: must, need to, got to, absolutely should, ought to.

CBT posits that these demands are at the core of psychological disturbance and emotional problems. They provoke unhealthy negative emotions such as anxiety, which in turn block creativity and limit our potential when it comes to goal achievement.

'Have to' and 'must' are rigid and inflexible

These inflexible demands that you impose on yourself, on other people or on the world, do not allow for the existence of other options such as not fulfilling your demand. They are viewed as 'non acceptance' beliefs.

For example, if you make a demand such as 'I have to succeed' or 'I must not fail', you are not allowing for the possibility that you might not succeed.

You can clearly see that by thinking in this rigid way you are essentially saying you do not have a choice. You are telling yourself, 'this is how it must be for me'.

Of course, some things do have to function in a certain way. The law of gravity means that if you drop a stone it will 'have to' fall down. We all 'have to' eat, drink, breathe and have shelter in order to survive. Otherwise we would die. And that is another 'have to' – we all 'have to' die at some point, whether we believe in an afterlife or not.

Most of the things that we believe are 'have to's are in fact wants or desires.

Exercise

List up to five important things in your life that you think you have to do.

Example: *I have to go to work.*

List up to five important things in your life that have to happen.

Example: *I have to be happy.*

List up to five important things in your life that must not happen.

Example: *I must not be alone.*

'Have to' and 'must' are not consistent with reality

'Have to' beliefs are not consistent with reality because in real life we sometimes do not get the things we insist on.

For example, if you hold the belief 'I must not make a mistake', you are essentially saying that it must never happen. Reality shows that everyone makes mistakes. That is the truth and you cannot escape from it by avoiding it, denying it or burying it. That's how it is even if you really dislike it.

The same applies to other demands you may make, such as other peoples' judgements of you: 'I have to be liked by people I meet.' Here reality will show you that while many people do like you, there will be some who might not. Insisting on being liked does not alter reality even if you hate it.

When you do not acknowledge or accept what the reality shows you, you are functioning solely in your own internal world or your version of reality. You are living in your head and refusing to acknowledge the truth of how things are.

'Have to' and 'must' are not logical

'Have to' and 'must' are not logical or based on common sense. They do not rationally follow from what you want and prefer.

If you reason that because you want something therefore it must happen, you show poor logic. It means everything that you want or desire HAS to happen. The interesting thing is that you probably have a lot of common sense, but sometimes you may let go of it when it concerns something you really want. In such cases you make yourself more vulnerable to the impact of unhealthy reasoning.

If you apply logic to the above example, then your desire would be to do well and not make a mistake. This is fair enough. It is healthy for you to have your own dreams, wants and likes. However, it would not make sense for you to demand that you have to get things right or that you must not make a mistake just because it is what you want. That would be poor reasoning.

Example

Consider the statement below. You can see that it is made up of two parts. Part one is the statement about your desire for something. Let's call that something 'xyz'. The second statement is a conclusion that follows from your first statement.

I want xyz ... AND THEREFORE I MUST HAVE xyz

Now replace xyz with 'the day to be nice and sunny'. Does your second statement sound reasonable?

I want the day to be nice and sunny ... AND THEREFORE the day MUST be nice and sunny.

Replace xyz with 'to get things right', or any other desire, and the same logic will apply. It is irrational to make the second demanding statement as this does not allow for the numerous other possibilities.

'Have to' and 'must' are not helpful

When you make an unreasonable and unrealistic demand on yourself, you will experience unhealthy negative emotions like anxiety, depression, guilt and so on.

In such a state your thinking becomes more negative and your assumptions tend to be untrue, unreasonable and limiting. Your behaviour is influenced by all of this. This means that you are more likely to react in an unhelpful way. This in turn impacts negatively on your performance and success, as shown in the diagram below.

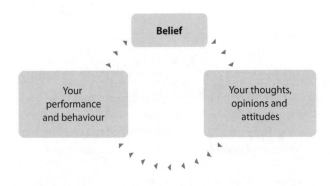

Example

Anne's goal is to feel confident and speak eloquently in staff meetings. She is anxious about whether she will remember what she wants to say when it's her turn to speak. She tells herself, 'you've got to remember when your turn comes; you have to calm down'. Her thoughts are about trying to remember at the same time as she is looking and counting how many people are ahead of her.

She becomes more insistent with her self-demand and the pressure to remember starts growing. She is no longer focused, in the moment, attentive to what is being discussed. She is completely in her own head. She notices her feelings of anxiety and worry are growing and begins to tell herself that she has to calm down. This creates more tension and pressure. Her heart is now beating rapidly, her palms are sweating and what she wants to do is get out of the meeting.

Her unrealistic demands do not help her. They are at the heart of her feelings of anxiety. She becomes focused on her internal state rather than on the meeting. She monitors herself, constantly checking when her turn is going to come. She feels her body experiencing the physical symptoms of anxiety and all she wants is for the meeting to stop.

Her demands do not help. They will not help her achieve her goal of speaking confidently and eloquently.

BAD VS AWFUL

How you judge the things you consider as 'bad' makes a big difference to how you feel. When you don't get what you want, you may judge that as bad. This judgement of 'badness' can be:

1. healthy, rational, realistic and logical or;
2. unhealthy, irrational, unrealistic and illogical.

CBT says that if you are not making a demand about the things you want, you will evaluate the badness of the situation in a realistic way that helps you move forward. However, if you are making a demand about what you want then you may evaluate or judge the badness in an unhealthy way that blocks you.

You will perceive the badness as if it is the worst thing that can happen to you or to any human being. This means you believe that nothing worse can happen. You may feel as if the world has ended. This is what we call 'awfulizing' or 'catastrophizing' the bad experience.

Think back to the example of the child who plays the piano: you will recall that her demand is that she must not make a mistake when she performs in front of her friends. Because she is demanding something that excludes the reality of making a mistake, it stands to reason that she may then view making a mistake as bad. Let's assume that she goes a step further and believes that making a mistake during her performance is the worst thing that can happen to her. She is now awfulizing. In her view there is nothing worse than making a mistake and she now believes this when she performs in front of an audience.

Of course, not everyone will see making a mistake as 'the end of the world'. However, there are certain events or some possibilities that you might feel are the worst things that might happen. This will affect how you feel, how you think and how you behave. All of these will influence your performance and potential to achieve your goals in a healthy way.

In CBT, awfulizing beliefs provoke unhealthy negative emotions and self-sabotaging behaviours.

Awfulizing beliefs are rigid and inflexible

When you see something as the worst possible thing that might happen, you are not allowing for the possibility that, actually, worse things can happen.

For example, if you believe you have to succeed because if you don't it would be awful, or even the end of the world, you are not allowing for the possibility that worse things than failure can happen.

You can see that making this sort of judgement about the badness of not succeeding is inflexible and rigid.

Nothing is the-end-of-the-world bad – apart from the end of the world itself, of course. For everything you believe is the worst possible scenario, I could suggest something worse. For everything I may view as the worst thing that could happen, you could suggest something worse. This concept could be controversial as you may be thinking of something very emotive, but when you allow yourself time to reflect, you will probably realize that there is always the possibility of something even worse – for example, the end of the world itself.

Exercise

List up to five important things in your life that you would view as the end of the world or the worst thing that could happen; for example, failing at something.

Now think of something worse for each one of your examples.

Awfulizing beliefs are not consistent with reality

It is not consistent with reality to view something as the worst thing that could happen. Clearly, something even worse could happen. You cannot prove that a worse thing could not happen. If you hold the belief 'I must not make a mistake because making a mistake would be awful' you are essentially saying that nothing worse than that is possible. If this was true, the world would have ended a long time ago because making a mistake would have been worse than a volcanic eruption.

Reality shows you that the world hasn't ended despite the fact that you made a mistake. So while making a mistake may be bad for you and possibly even for other people, it is still not the worst thing that might happen.

You may argue that to you it is the worst thing that could happen. But think about how that alters your view of yourself, others or the world. What consequences does it have for your life and performance?

This doesn't mean you should deny that bad things do happen, but remember not to turn that badness into the end of the world.

Awfulizing beliefs are not logical

It does not make sense to awfulize the things you view as bad. You may think, 'well, I'm not logical and that's just me' or, 'if I want to make something the worst thing then I will'. You have every right to think exactly as you wish. You may think in a reasoned and logical way about the bad things or you may think in the opposite way – that is your choice. Your conclusions and reasoning can be right or wrong. That reasoning will impact on how you feel and perform though.

You may understand logic and reasoned thinking, but when you let go of it you may find you are vulnerable to reasoning in unhealthy and wrong ways about your situation, yourself and your abilities.

Example

The statement below is made up of two parts. Part one acknowledges that something is bad. Let's call that something 'xyz'. The second statement makes a conclusion that follows from the first statement.

> *Xyz is bad ... AND THEREFORE xyz is the end of the world (or awful, or terrible, or a catastrophe; the worst thing possible).*
>
> Now if you replaced xyz with 'a rainy cold day', does your second statement sound reasonable?
>
> *A rainy cold day is bad ... AND THEREFORE a rainy cold day is the end of the world.*
>
> Replace xyz with 'making a mistake', and the same logic will apply. Logically it is wrong to make a catastrophic conclusion from the first part of the statement.

Awfulizing beliefs are not helpful

If you turn the badness of an event or a possible event into the worst thing that has happened or could happen, this awfulizing belief will provoke you to feel unhealthy tension and stress. If you view something as terrible or awful, you will experience unhealthy negative emotions like anxiety, rage or guilt. Your body responds to what you believe whether it is true or not, so if you believe making a mistake is terrible you will feel anxious about making mistakes. In this state of anxiety your thoughts will be negative and your behaviour will be unhelpful. You cannot expect to be at your best when you think in this way.

This can create a circular loop in your thinking; for example, 'it would be awful if I made a mistake and so I must not make a mistake' or, 'I must get things right because it would be terrible if I didn't'. As a result, you will be watching and waiting to make a mistake, which in turn impacts your focus and concentration.

Awfulizing in this way provokes thoughts and feelings that are unhealthy. It limits what you can achieve and creates harmful physiological symptoms.

Example

Let's go back to the earlier example of the woman whose goal is to feel confident and speak eloquently in staff meetings. She feels anxious about remembering what she wants to say. She imposes a demand on herself to remember because she views going blank as the worst thing that could happen to her. She continues to insist that she has to remember because if she doesn't it would be awful, even catastrophic. She feels the anxiety provoked by both the demand she is making and by the fact that she sees going blank not just as bad but as TERRIBLE. As she notices her anxiety she starts to demand that she MUST calm down: 'Oh, I'm anxious, this is horrible. I MUST calm down.' This in turn produces even more anxiety.

She is looking around at her colleagues and all her thoughts are about how terrible it would be if she didn't remember and how awful it will be if she can't calm herself down in time. She is now in a state of desperation and all she wants to do is to get out of that meeting room. She is totally engaged in her catastrophic thoughts and in her own head. Her pulse is racing and she can feel the blood pressure rising.

Her rigid and catastrophizing belief will not help her achieve her goal of confident and eloquent speech.

There are, of course, times when anxiety is healthy. For example if our lives are in real danger, anxiety causes adrenaline to pump through our bodies to prepare for the fight or flight. So if making a mistake is believed to be life-threatening, the body will react in the same way: with anxiety and fear.

DIFFICULT VS UNBEARABLE

What you believe about the things you find difficult affects how you feel and influences to a great degree the choices you make. It impacts how you think and behave and ultimately affects your performance. Let's look more closely at the things you find difficult.

When you don't get what you want or desire or when you think about not getting what you want and desire, you may judge that as difficult or frustrating; for example, when you don't get your own way or when you cannot resolve a problem immediately. How you judge such difficulties or frustrations can be either healthy or unhealthy. A healthy judgement will tend to be rational, logical and realistic. An unhealthy judgement will tend to be irrational, unrealistic and illogical.

When you are not making a demand about what you want and don't get what you want, your judgement of such a difficulty will be realistic, healthy and problem-solving, and will help you to move forward. However, if you make a demand about what you want and don't get what you demand, your judgement of such a frustration and difficulty will be unhealthy and unhelpful: you will feel stuck. Remember that demands lead to you feeling as if you do not have any choice at all, creating a sense of being forced into doing something.

In effect, you make the difficulty 'unbearable'. You will probably use expressions like 'I can't cope', 'I can't stand it', 'it's unbearable'. In CBT we call this a 'Low Frustration Tolerance' (LFT) belief. You believe you are not capable of bearing the frustration or the difficulty of not getting what you are demanding.

Think back to the example of the child who plays the piano. She was already creating considerable anxiety by demanding that she absolutely must not make a mistake during her performance. Her body and mind were acting as if someone was forcing her to play the piano in front of her friends. In such a state, it is easy to understand she may also believe making a mistake would be UNBEARABLE to her. In her view, making a mistake would be something she would not be able to tolerate or stand. This third belief about not tolerating mistakes provokes further anxiety and adds to her worries.

It is possible that you have all three unhealthy beliefs about certain things in your life. For example, you may make a demand about how certain people drive on the road; you may tell yourself it's awful that they drive that badly and how unbearable you find it. This type of thinking can leads to irrational anger or even road rage. You may also view bad driving as terrible but tolerate it. Or you may not find it terrible but definitely feel like you cannot stand it. In other words you may have both the catastrophizing belief and the LFT about certain things, or you may just have one of them, as a result of your demands. LFT beliefs provoke unhealthy negative emotions, thoughts and self-sabotaging behaviours.

LFT beliefs are rigid and inflexible

When you make the difficulty or frustration you are experiencing 'unbearable' or 'intolerable', you are not allowing for the possibility – or even the fact – that you can tolerate it, or indeed that you are tolerating it.

For example, if you hold the belief 'I have to succeed because if I don't it will be unbearable' then you are not allowing for the fact that you have accepted it and still are tolerating it.

You can easily see that believing you cannot stand or tolerate something is inflexible and rigid. When you think about it, believing something is unbearable does not leave you any room for improvement. Your body's responses, emotions, thoughts and behaviour will be a consequence of what you tell yourself about the difficulty.

Exercise

List up to five important things in your life that you believe were unbearable for you, for example: it was unbearable when my relationship ended.

List up to five important things that you believe you would not be able to cope with, for example: I couldn't cope with confrontation.

Despite the fact that you have felt some things were unbearable, you are still here, reading this. What does this fact tell you about your resiliency?

LFT beliefs are not consistent with reality

It is not consistent with reality to believe that something is unbearable when you are still here to talk about it. When you tell yourself something is intolerable or unbearable you almost believe that you would cease to exist if that situation or event actually happened.

For example, if you hold the belief, 'I must not make a mistake because making a mistake would be unbearable', this means that mistakes are something you could not survive. If this were true, none of us would be alive because we have all made mistakes.

Reality shows that you do tolerate making mistakes even if you find it very hard to do so. Reality shows that you still manage to get up, make a cup of tea, shower, do your work and carry on functioning. It shows that as long as you are alive and breathing you can cope with the thing that you have been telling yourself is unbearable. I have had many clients who initially believed that going through a divorce was unbearable but they survived it. We convince ourselves of these things, even if they are not true, instead of reminding ourselves of the reality and the truth about our strength and resilience in tolerating difficulties.

If you are going through a difficult time right now, acknowledge that you are experiencing difficulties and frustrations. But do not give up on the reality that you are tolerating whatever is happening, proved by the fact that you are still alive and reading this book.

LFT beliefs are not logical

It is not logical to conclude that something is unbearable, just because it is very or even extremely difficult, when you are still alive and breathing. Your feelings will be provoked by such thoughts. This is important to think about, because sometimes faulty thinking becomes so effortless and habitual that you just accept it without question. You do not have to like logic but it is in your best interest to use common sense. You have lots of common sense and it is going to be up to you to identify your faulty thinking because there is something in it for you.

Example

Consider the statement below. You can see that it is made up of two parts. Part one acknowledges that something is difficult or frustrating. Let's call that difficulty 'xyz'. The second statement is about the conclusion that follows from the first statement.

Xyz is difficult ... AND THEREFORE xyz is unbearable (or intolerable, or I can't stand it or I can't cope with it).

When you replace the xyz with 'a rainy, cold day', does the second statement sound reasonable?

A rainy cold day is frustrating ... AND THEREFORE a rainy, cold day is unbearable.

Replace xyz with 'making a mistake', and the same logic will apply. It remains logically wrong to make the second LFT statement a conclusion that flows from the first.

LFT beliefs are not helpful

When you believe that the difficulties in your life are unbearable, your body functions differently as a result. LFT beliefs have consequences. They are not harmless or healthy. Believing that you can't stand something will provoke emotions such as anxiety, depression, rage and shame. Your thoughts about your abilities will be negative and your problem-solving skills will be weakened. In a state of anxiety, provoked by your LFT belief, you will not be functioning at your best. Your performance will be greatly affected.

LFT beliefs make you work in a restricted way and create unhealthy tension in your body. It's as if you are walking under a very low ceiling. The more you lower your tolerance, the more you lower this ceiling. The solution is, of course, to learn to deal with, and increase your tolerance to, difficulties.

Example

Let us return to the woman whose goal is to feel confident and speak eloquently in staff meetings. Imagine that she now has an LFT belief about the state of her anxiety. She tells herself that she can't stand her feelings and that they are unbearable, as well as being horrible. This LFT belief is likely to further reinforce her demand to get rid of her anxiety, but it does the opposite. She is so intolerant of the sensations of anxiety that she feels them more, not less. This happens because she is now so sensitive to the emotion itself. Her mind is even more focused on her feelings and not on the meeting. She is now completely absorbed in her own world. Her low tolerance to anxiety is lowering the ceiling she is under. All she feels like doing is – you've guessed it – getting out of that meeting.

Her rigid intolerant belief is not helping her achieve her goal of confidence and eloquent speech. In fact, it will cause her throat to dry and her mind to focus on running away. As the body is now geared for the flight response, the energy used for recall is diverted to this function. Her body is reacting as if her colleagues are a pride of lions looking at her and seeing lunch. If there was a pride of lions, that is if she was actually under threat, then her body would gear into anxiety. It would divert the energy of many physical and mental functions to those that would be useful for running away. So in a state of anxiety she would not be geared up to presenting sales figures. Her rigid, catastrophizing, LFT beliefs would make her body and mind respond as if she was facing a pride of lions.

SELF-ACCEPTANCE VS SELF-DAMNING

How you judge yourself when you do not get what you want is very important. This is about how you rate yourself when your desires are not met or when you fail to achieve your goals. How you rate yourself, or what you tell yourself and believe about yourself, makes a big difference to how you feel, think and behave. It greatly influences how well you perform and how happily and healthily you achieve your goals.

When you do not get what you want, you may judge that as failure; you have failed to get what you want. In reality, you may not always get things right – which is not the same as 'failing to' get things right. What you conclude about yourself as a result of this can be either healthy or unhealthy:

- A healthy conclusion would be rational, realistic and logical.
- An unhealthy conclusion would be irrational, unrealistic and illogical.

When your belief about yourself is healthy and realistic it will help you to move forward, be problem-solving and constructive. It sets you up for achieving your goals. It also encourages you to get up and have another go or do things differently after disappointment or failure. It may provoke you to feel upset or unhappy for a short period of time, because you have not been successful at getting what you want, but you learn from the experience and move on.

If your belief about yourself is unhealthy and unhelpful, you will put yourself down because you have not achieved what you wanted. In effect you turn the disappointment you experienced into an indication and proof of how bad, stupid or worthless you are. You believe things like 'I'm a failure because I failed', 'I'm worthless because I was rejected', 'I'm useless because I couldn't think of a solution' and so on. In CBT we call this a 'self-damning' belief. It means you rate yourself as a human being based on whether or not your demand was met.

Think back to the example of the child who plays the piano. She was already demanding that she must not make a mistake when she performs because doing so in front of everyone would be awful and unbearable. You already understand that such beliefs are unhealthy because they are rigid, unrealistic, illogical and unhelpful. They provoke anxiety and negative thinking. Now imagine that, as she sits down to do more practice, this belief is triggered because she is thinking about her performance. In her state of anxiety she will begin to focus on how she is playing all the time, instead of practising. This means she will disconnect from the music because she is in her own head assessing how she is playing and being hyper-vigilant. In this state the likelihood of making mistakes increases and she starts to notice that she is making mistakes. She then starts to believe that she is 'useless' because she keeps making mistakes. As this negative thought is entertained and repeated she starts to believe it, and before long she is making herself more anxious because she now thinks a useless person like herself will be playing in front of the whole school. She then makes more demands to get things right, and the unhealthy chain of her demand is now linked to the catastrophizing belief, LFT and self-damning belief.

Her overall belief now is:

- *I must not make a mistake when I play in front of the whole school and my friends. If I make a mistake:*
  - *It would be the end of the world.*
  - *I would not cope.*
  - *It would prove that I'm useless.*

It's easy to see how self-damning beliefs are at heart of unhealthy negative emotions, thoughts and self-sabotaging behaviours.

Self-damning beliefs are rigid and inflexible

Self-damning beliefs are rigid and inflexible because they let you to see yourself in one way and as a direct reflection of your negative goal or negative behaviour. No allowance is made for you to be anything else apart from 'useless', 'bad', 'worthless' or a 'failure'. You become your failure. You become your negative behaviour.

For example, if you hold the belief, 'I have to succeed because if I don't it proves that I'm a failure', you are not allowing or acknowledging the things that you are still succeeding at, for example breathing, washing, holding down a job, having friends and probably lots of other things as well. You are making a judgement about your entire self based on the one thing that you are focused on.

You can see how rigid and inflexible you can be about yourself when you criticize yourself in this way.

You may think, 'well, I am a failure because what I wanted was very important to me; it defined me'. I will respond by saying you are more than that important thing you defined yourself by. You are a million and one things. You are all of your biological and psychological traits and tendencies. You may be a brother, a sister, a father, an uncle, an aunt, a friend, a cook, or a football-loving, cricket-hating, barn-dancing person as well. You are more than just one thing that you define yourself by.

Rating yourself as totally bad or worthless is so rigid that it triggers your body and your mind to feel the consequences of such a label or belief.

Self-damning is inconsistent with reality

It is not consistent with reality to believe that you are a total failure if you do not get what you are demanding. While you can show that you may have done badly, or that you may have failed at achieving what you were insisting on, you would not be able to prove that, as a result, you have now become a total failure as a human being. You can prove that you failed but not that you are a failure. You can prove that someone rejected you but not that you are now worthless as a person. When you believe you are a failure, by taking this to a logical conclusion you should be able to prove that from the moment you failed you continued to fail at everything else, including breathing.

For example, if you hold the belief, 'I must get my promotion because if I don't it would prove that I'm worthless' then you are effectively believing that you have no value at all. Everything about you becomes worthless from that moment on. You become a failure at everything in life.

Reality shows that you succeed at most things, and fail at some things. Reality shows that you are liked by many people, disliked by some and neither liked nor disliked by others. Reality shows that sometimes you make mistakes, other times you get things right. Reality shows that sometimes you perform brilliantly, sometimes badly, and at all of the standards in between. Reality shows that it is your performance and behaviour that vary, not your worth. But if you rate your worthiness by your performance then you will feel the consequences of it.

If you believe that as a result of failing your examination you become a failure as a person, then why are you not failing at everything? If you become a failure because of something in particular, then surely you become a failure at everything. So it is not true that you are a failure if you fail.

Again, you may say, 'but if I "feel" like a failure then surely I am one'. However, your feelings are not an indication of the truth. Your feelings are triggered by how you are thinking. If your thinking is unhealthy, unrealistic or illogical then your feelings will be the result of such thinking.

Acknowledge that you are imperfect, because that is all your failures show, and that you are human and fallible like everyone else. Imagine that everything about you is represented by all the different fruits in a basket. The apple represents your failure at getting that promotion. Would you say that all the other fruit is ruined and should be thrown in the rubbish bin?

You may ask, 'if my worth is not dependent on my behaviour and performance or on anything at all, then what is it dependent on?' Your worth is not dependent on anything. You are a worthwhile but imperfect human being just because you breathe. I often explain this by asking whether, when you look at a new baby, you question the worth of his or her life? Do you think that the loving parents look at their baby and think, 'he's worthwhile BUT he becomes a total failure if he is rejected by his first girlfriend, and he becomes worthless if someone doesn't like him'? You wouldn't consider such thinking because you know it sounds so ridiculous and untrue. But you sometimes believe it about yourself.

What do you think about some of the truths you have believed until now?

Self-damning beliefs are not logical

It is not logical to conclude that you are a totally worthless person because you did not succeed or because you failed at something. This is an example of flawed common sense. It is a faulty leap of logic. If you fail, the logical conclusion to make about yourself is that it proves you are not perfect, not that you are a total failure as a person.

Example

Consider the statement below. You can see that it is made up of two parts. Part one acknowledges that you failed at something. Let's call that something 'xyz'. The second statement is about the conclusion that follows from the first statement.

I failed at xyz ... AND THEREFORE I AM a failure as a person.

Replace xyz with 'getting things right' and the same logic will apply. It remains logically wrong to make the second statement.

I failed at getting things right ... AND THEREFORE I AM a failure as a person.

Self-damning beliefs are not helpful

It's easy to see that there are no benefits in rating yourself as 'worthless' or 'useless' or a 'failure' because of something – even a number of things – that have gone wrong in your life. When you make this huge leap from failing to achieve something (whether it is an exam, a promotion, a relationship – or even when you fail to remain calm and relaxed) to believing that you are a failure as a person, your body and mind will be affected by these beliefs.

Damning yourself in such a negative way is not only untrue and makes no sense at all, but it will also have unfortunate consequences. This sort of belief triggers anxiety and depression, may provoke you to feel irrationally angry with yourself and with other people and with life in general, and may also lead to other unhealthy emotions.

I'm sure that there have been many times in your life when you have rated yourself in such a totally negative way. You may even hold such beliefs at the moment. You know how they leave you feeling and how they affect your thinking. You also know that they create this negative cycle of thinking, doing and believing as shown by the diagram on page 44.

Self-damning beliefs limit your abilities and your potential. If, for example, you believe that you are 'useless' because of something that you can't do or couldn't do last time you tried, like making a presentation, you know that by just thinking about standing up in public your negative self-doubting thoughts immediately creep into your mind and your heart starts to race.

The healthy way to handle this sort of situation is to:

- accept yourself as a worthwhile but fallible person; or
- just rate your behaviour and performance and stop at that.

At this moment you may think 'it all sounds good but how do I do this?' The 'how' will come soon.

Example

Think back to the woman whose goal is to feel confident and to speak eloquently in staff meetings. She feels anxious about remembering what she wants to say. She also has catastrophizing beliefs and LFT beliefs.

Imagine that she also has a self-damning belief linked to her demand about remembering, so she believes that her inability to remember is proof that she is a 'useless' person.

Now other thoughts about herself, not just about her abilities, start to invade her mind, creating further feelings of anxiety and tension in her body. Her body responds to the self-damning beliefs, making her heart rate go up and her muscles tense. As she notices this, her second belief about anxiety also kicks in.

Now imagine that she goes on to damn herself more because she cannot control her feelings of anxiety. So being anxious is now further proof of how useless she is. This vicious cycle is preoccupying her mind and distancing her even further from being at the meeting. In such a state, her body and mind are definitely not set up for remembering what to say when her turn comes to speak. She feels like escaping from it all.

THE CONCEPTS AT THE HEART OF HEALTHY BELIEFS

If your unhealthy beliefs are rigid and inflexible, untrue, illogical and unhelpful, then your healthy beliefs will be flexible, true, logical and helpful to you.

Healthy beliefs are based on the union between your internal world view and external reality. That means your healthy beliefs are balanced.

Essentially, healthy beliefs will help you focus and strive for goals and to plan for the worst, rather than avoid the possibility of having to face the worst.

Want to but I don't have to

Instead of the coercive 'MUST', a healthy belief is based on a WANT or desire coupled with an acceptance or acknowledgement of what external reality can sometimes show us. The 'have to' is taken out of the equation.

Example

I want the day to be nice and sunny when I wake up but that does not mean that it has to be.

Or:

I'd like the day to be nice and sunny but I ACCEPT that there is a chance that it might not be.

So you focus on your desire but not in a coercive and demanding way.

Bad but not the end of the world

Instead of awfulizing the badness as if the world has ended, you accept that something bad has happened. However, as bad as it is, it is still not the end of the world. Once again this is a union between your internal view that something bad has happened and external reality, which shows that the world has not ended.

Example

It's bad that today is not nice and sunny but it's not the end of the world.

Or:

I don't like it that the day is not as I want but it's not awful.

Difficult but not unbearable

Instead of making difficulties unbearable, a healthy belief acknowledges your internal view that you are experiencing a difficulty. It also acknowledges that you are still alive and here to tell the tale.

Example

I find it difficult when the day is not nice and sunny but I can tolerate it.

Or:

I am worthwhile but I am fallible.

A healthy belief is based on accepting yourself unconditionally. This means you do not rate yourself at all; you rate your behaviour and your performance. As a human being you are complex and made up of positive, negative and neutral qualities. A negative quality does not negate the rest of you, so a healthy belief acknowledges that you do sometimes make mistakes because you are fallible. It does not say that you are a mistake – in fact, it acknowledges the whole you as neither good nor bad, but as someone who sometimes does good and sometimes does bad. It acknowledges that you are a worthwhile but imperfect human being.

Example

If I make a mistake it doesn't mean I am a failure. I am fallible but remain worthwhile. My worth does not depend on whether I make a mistake or not.

Exercise

What would you be able to do better if you did not put yourself down or rate yourself as worthless?

How would an attitude of 'I want to but I don't have to' affect how you feel and how you go about doing things?

What do you think you would be able to achieve if you did not catastrophize failing?

3
Setting Your Goals

This chapter is about setting personally motivating goals after a period of self-reflection. You will learn how to use words that create vivid, emotive pictures in your mind of what you want to achieve.

REFLECT ON WHAT YOU WANT

Once you have accepted the principle of emotional responsibility, what you can achieve becomes possible.

If the idea that you are responsible for how you feel is daunting, make a note of your feelings for the time being and carry on reading. If, however, it feels like a window opening, you may be getting a sense of freedom and excitement. Knowing that you are responsible for your feelings and for your life means that there is a way to create change.

You have perhaps begun to understand that your beliefs are at the heart of your emotions, thoughts and behaviour. Your beliefs, thoughts, emotions and behaviours all influence and feed off each other so you condition yourself and reinforce what you think about yourself and your abilities.

You also know that there is a different, healthy way of thinking – a healthy version of your unhealthy beliefs. The healthy beliefs are flexible, true and consistent with reality, they make sense and they are helpful to you.

Now you may start reflecting on what you want to achieve or how you want your life to be.

The first thing is to scan your life for what matters to you. You can do this by creating your own balance wheel to reflect all the key areas in your life in a broad and general way. You do not need to be specific at this stage. It is about looking at the overall big picture.

Your balance wheel

The circle below represents some of the significant areas in your life. It is by no means an exhaustive list. For example, you may wish to include a section for retirement instead of career or education and add a spiritual or political section. This circle can include any areas you like. You may already know what your goals are, but you may want to think about other areas too.

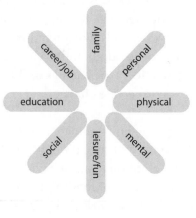

For each area of your life, rate your level of satisfaction between 0 and 10. Zero represents the worst in terms of happiness and 10 represents complete contentment. If there is no room for improvement at present, this shows that this particular area is not a priority for you.

Family

Family life can be a source of great happiness or it can be full of emotional, behavioural and communication problems. If your family life is important to you, it is worth reflecting on this area. Problems in families may be due to past unresolved issues, or difficulties in forgiving someone's behaviour. There may be present difficulties, such as financial stress, which impact on communication and mood, and worries about the future, such as fears about children leaving home and the consequences of that on your relationship.

Family issues may also be about closeness and a feeling that you could be closer. They may be about your relationship with your parents or a recognition that you may want to do more, for example visiting more often, and the emotional consequences of that.

Level of satisfaction = ___/10

Personal

This area may be about your relationships, or any other personal difficulties you may have; for example, shyness or feelings of anxiety when you are socializing. It may be about worrying about rejection when you go on a date or it may be about stopping smoking.

It could also be about your personal development. Personal development may involve learning about yourself, making peace with the past and moving on, understanding yourself, or gaining insight and learning about your psychological health.

Level of satisfaction = ___/10

Physical
This is about assessing how satisfied you are with your physical health or your body shape and weight. Your physical health may be one of the areas you wish to change. You may wish to exercise more or lose weight. You may have dreams about running a marathon. This may be the time to start thinking and implementing your ideas.

Level of satisfaction = ___/10

Mental
The area of mental health is one where many people now seek professional help. Knowing when you need help and looking for it is in itself an excellent goal. Do you tend to suffer from depression or anxiety to such an extent that it often interrupts your life? Maybe you are suffering from problems like self-loathing, panic disorder or obsessive compulsive disorder? Mental health problems are common and speaking to your GP first is highly recommended.

Mental health is also about how you feel generally. For example, you may wish to be calmer and more positive in your thinking. Maybe you have always wanted to see the glass half full but cannot quite manage it. Maybe you have tried to be positive but weren't quite able to stay that way and want to know why.

Level of satisfaction = ___/10

Leisure/fun

You may feel that you want to have more fun in your life, but how much time do you set aside for leisure activities? You may have devoted more time to having fun when you were younger but work, family or financial commitments may have meant that it became less of a priority over time. You may want to commit more time to this area of your life because all work and no play is not as fulfilling as it used to be.

It is not uncommon to be doing well and striving for the things that you want, but noticing that perhaps you are not smiling as much as you used to. Maybe most of your friends are now married and the things they want to do have changed but you still want to socialize more or be engaged in more leisurely activities.

Level of satisfaction = ___/10

Social

How is your social life and how satisfied are you with it? You may have been focused on your career, on your family life or even on your education in such an intense way that this area of your life has been neglected. If you know you have done this as a conscious choice and feel happy with reducing the priority of your social life that's fine, but do you find yourself working late and not having time to return your friends' calls? Have they stopped calling because you are always too busy to accept social invitations? Do you feel that you are neglecting this part of your life and that you are unhappy about it? Maybe you have moved jobs and find yourself away from most of your friends and the idea of making new friends feels too much like hard work?

Level of satisfaction = ___/10

Education

You may have started work quite young and now that you are more settled you are thinking about returning to education. It could be that you want to continue with your higher education in order to get a more satisfying career. Whatever your reason, you have started to think about it. Perhaps you are surprised at yourself because you are now thinking that education could be fun but fear doing it. At this stage do not allow your feelings to stop your thoughts. You are not committing to anything. Just reflect on this area and assess whether you feel it has become important to you.

Level of satisfaction = ___/10

Career/job

You often hear that most people are not totally happy with their careers, and that many people are opting for self-employment or changing their jobs. Are you feeling dissatisfied with your job, especially if you spend at least seven hours a day doing it?

How do you feel about your work? What do you think about your career? Is this what you imagined yourself doing when you were younger? Are you unsure about what you want to do but know that this is not it?

Level of satisfaction = ___/10

Tip: If you have identified areas other than those listed above, remember to rate your level of satisfaction in these additional areas also.

Importance of what you want

It's easy to see how important it is to reflect on all of this as part of your overall scheme of things. It is almost impossible to achieve goals if they are not important or if you do not get some personal benefit from them. The previous section helped you to scan your life and reflect on your current position, that is where you are now. It was about being honest with yourself about your current level of satisfaction and thinking about how badly you want to change it.

You can be dissatisfied with one area of your life but tolerate it because your focus is on another part that you feel is more important at the moment. Your goal is your vision of the future that you want. It is a vision that you care about. It should provoke an emotion when you think about it: either a positive one, indicating that you have a healthy positive attitude about it or a negative one because you have unhealthy beliefs about yourself. Remember that ABC model?

A stands for the trigger or event

B stands for beliefs – either healthy or unhealthy

C stands for consequence – emotions, thoughts, behaviours and symptoms

Achieving or not achieving your goal would be the trigger, or A.

Your belief about yourself, or your skills when you think about your goal, or the problem you are having with it is B.

Your feelings, thoughts and what you see yourself doing is C.

If your belief (B) about yourself, others or the world when you think about your goal (A) is healthy, then your emotions (C) will be positive and constructive, but if your belief is unhealthy then your feelings will be destructive.

If you say that you want something but do not feel anything about it when you imagine it, then perhaps you need time to reflect on how important it is for you at this stage in your life.

Exercise

Go back to your balance wheel and look at the areas of your life that you are currently dissatisfied with or the areas that you want to improve. For each of these areas:

1. Rate your current level of satisfaction.
2. Rate your preferred level of satisfaction.
3. Finally, prioritize them in order of importance so number 1 is the most important area in your life and so on.

SETTING SMART GOALS

Goals reflect the way you want things to be. They are your desires, the things that you want to happen, the dreams you wish to fulfil. You are constantly setting goals and keeping an eye on the things that are going to happen in the future, like birthdays, anniversaries or other important events. Human beings are naturally goal-oriented.

You set goals from the moment you wake up, such as going to work and getting there on time. You may have lunchtime goals, social goals, supermarket and clothes-shopping goals. All of these activities are about visualizing something in the future, then moving towards it and making it happen. Having the ability to focus, imagine and visualize the goal in a vivid way helps you move forward.

The more significant your goal, the stronger its pulling power. So how do you make your goal vivid and colourful so that you can imagine it? Think about something that you have looked forward to in the past, for example planning a party or going on holiday. You start thinking about a holiday, then you work out where, when and how much you want to spend. Do you want to go in July, August or September? You start looking through brochures or searching on the internet.

By the time you have completed your plans, your holiday goal has become **SMART**: Specific, Measurable, Achievable, Realistic, Time-oriented. Now you can visualize it and imagine yourself relaxing by the pool or skiing down snowy slopes, having drinks at sunset or enjoying a nice meal. You may be planning how one day you will go to the beach and the day after go on an excursion. You are now focused on your goal. What's the likelihood that after a week or so of this focused thinking you will be booking your holiday?

SMART goals help you visualize the end result more clearly and vividly.

Specific

Specific means that your goal is clear, so it is about the where, how and what. A specific goal gives you a clear picture of the outcome. Simply wanting a salary increase is not specific, it is only specific if you talk about how much of an increase you are looking for.

The more you concentrate on making your goal specific, the better you will visualize it and strive towards it. Remember that you are naturally goal directed.

Measurable

Goals need to be measurable so that you can assess how well you have done and what you still need to do to improve on your result. It is important that your goals are clear and tangible as this means that there will be proof that you are achieving – or not achieving – your goal in some way. For example, if you plan to lose weight and have the specific goal of wanting to lose 1 stone, you can check that you are moving towards your goal by weighing yourself. You will have evidence to measure.

Achievable

Your goal needs to be achievable rather than based on wishful thinking. For example, you may hope to win the lottery and think that by carrying out some ritual it becomes achievable. You may say, 'what if that was possible?' Just look at the results. Is this what reality shows you? Millions of people spend time doing the lottery but most will not be successful.

Achievable goals have to be attainable and feasible. How feasible is what you want?

Realistic

Realistic goals are sensible. They tend to be based on fact and the reality of life. This doesn't mean that you should downgrade your desires, but do ask yourself if they are realistic. Unrealistic goals, ideas and expectations tend to have the words always, never, or all the time in them. They are irrational. For example, wanting never to feel anxious again is just not realistic. Always wanting to be happy or wanting everyone to like you are two common examples of irrational goals, as is wanting to always have the feeling of being in love, despite 20 years of marriage.

You may want to lose 2 stone in weight. On the face of it sounds achievable, but if you wanted that to happen in one week it becomes unrealistic.

Time-oriented

This is about how long you think it will take you to reach your goal. It is good to focus on time because this provides the energy and motivation you need to be healthy and realistic about what you want to achieve. You might start putting unreasonable pressure on yourself to achieve something instead of reviewing your time frame. Without a time element, you might lose focus and allow yourself to drift away from what you want. Focusing on time indicates that you are ready to commit to it.

Achieving your goals depends on whether you have healthy beliefs about yourself and your skills – which will help you achieve them – or unhealthy beliefs that will stop you from moving towards them positively.

When you put all the **SMART** elements together you start to create a vivid, 'all singing, all dancing' goal. If your goal fails on any of the **SMART** categories then it is no longer **SMART** and you need to go back and modify it.

A **SMART** goal sets you up for success, and your healthy beliefs provide the energy and drive for you to move towards it.

Exercise

Look back to the last exercise where you rated your level of satisfaction in the different areas of your life and prioritized them in the context of your bigger picture. Choose one significant area that you are unsatisfied with.

Reflect on this important area and think about how you want it to be for you.

Write down your **SMART** goal about your significant choice. Ensure it meets all the **SMART** criteria.

CURRENT GOAL-SABOTAGING BELIEFS

When you set a goal that is significant to you, a number of things can happen.

- You may start to create pictures and images in your head.
- You may start having an internal dialogue about yourself or your abilities.
- You may start to have feelings or emotions.
- You may start doing something or feeling like you want to do something.
- You may start to get physiological sensations in your body.
- You may experience all or any combination of these things.

If you want to achieve something but find you are not succeeding, something is stopping you. The easiest way to gain insight into this blockage is to check your emotions and thoughts when you imagine your goal.

Think back to what you learned about your different emotions, the healthy negative ones and the unhealthy negative ones.

In the CBT model, unhealthy emotions are triggered by unhealthy beliefs.

When you imagine something, or think about what you want to do, you may experience different emotions. This can be quite confusing. For example, thinking about your goal might trigger feelings of anxiety (unhealthy) about whether you will succeed, or guilt about taking time away from your family (unhealthy), or concern (healthy) about the work that it may involve.

Taking a systematic, sensible approach is one of the best ways of understanding these varied emotions. This is all with the aim of identifying your goal-sabotaging beliefs at this point. Later on, you will learn how to change them in order to free yourself from their grip.

Using the ABC framework to keep the model in mind will help you identify your various emotions and thoughts.

Example

Jane is a 35-year-old married woman with two children. Her husband is a self-employed electrician and she works in the Human Resources department of a corporate company. An opportunity has arisen to do a part-time diploma course in psychology, which her company will fund, and it's a subject she's always been interested in. The application form has a due date three months from now. Jane has been avoiding filling in the application form, as she is in a dilemma as to whether she should apply. She wants to do it but her feelings and thoughts are negative. She is wondering whether she could manage it and is scared about the potential hard work. She is also anxious about how she would feel if the work meant that she would be spending a few nights a week studying, instead of being with her children and husband.

Jane's goal

Jane has a goal to apply for a diploma in psychology.

This is a **SMART** goal. Why?

Jane's emotions and thoughts

She feels anxiety rather than concern because her thoughts are negative and her behaviour is avoidant. What is she anxious about?

Jane's ABC

In Jane's case, the 'A' in the ABC – the event or trigger – is applying for the diploma in psychology. Her goal triggers her feelings of anxiety.

Her feelings of anxiety are the emotional consequences. These are the 'C' in the ABC.

A	B	C
I'm thinking about applying for a diploma in psychology and it might be hard	→B	→Anxiety
How will I feel if it means time away from my family?	→B	→Guilt

Since Jane has two states of anxiety, she will have two unhealthy anxiety-provoking beliefs – one per state. She is also likely to have a belief that would trigger guilt. So she should be working to change three unhealthy beliefs in this example.

Exercise

STEP 1 IDENTIFY YOUR SMART GOAL

Start by writing down your SMART goal on a piece of paper.

STEP 2 IDENTIFY YOUR UNHEALTHY NEGATIVE EMOTIONS

What are you experiencing emotionally when you think about your goal? (You may write 'stressed', 'upset' or other expressions of emotion.)

Write down the negative unhealthy emotions that are blocking you from achieving your goal. (Go back to Chapter 1 and use the tables about emotions to help you clarify them.)

Now construct your 'A' and 'C' in the ABC ('A' is the trigger of the emotion, 'B' is the unknown belief, 'C' is the emotion). Triggers can be thoughts, sensations or events about the past, present or future. They can also be images and pictures.

IDENTIFYING YOUR CURRENT SABOTAGING BELIEFS

So far you have identified 'A' and 'C' in the ABC model.

The next step is to identify the 'B' in the ABC model. The easiest way to identify these beliefs is by imagining or thinking about the trigger, focusing on the emotion you feel, asking yourself a number of questions and writing down the answer for each question.

What type of questions do you ask?

1. To identify the demand belief you ask:
    What do my feelings tell me about what I'm demanding/insisting on when I'm thinking about my problem? What am I saying MUST or MUST NOT happen?
2. To identify the catastrophizing belief you ask:
    What do my feelings tell me about the badness of not having my demand met? Are they telling me it's bad but not the end of the world or awful, terrible, horrible, the end of the world?
3. To identify the low frustration tolerance belief you ask:
    What do my feelings tell me about the difficulty and frustration of not having my demand met? Are they telling me it's difficult (hard, tough, frustrating) or unbearable (can't cope, can't stand it, can't tolerate it)?
4. **To identify the self-damning, other-damning or world-damning belief you ask:**
    What do my feelings tell me about how I judge myself or others as a consequence of not having my demand met? Are they telling me that I failed but that I'm not a failure or are they telling me that I'm a failure (worthless, useless, loser, rubbish, bad, weak)?

Jane's ABC in the previous example:
Jane identifies the 'B' in the first ABC

Jane thinks about applying for the diploma course, which might turn out to be very hard. She focuses on her feeling of anxiety. She then asks:

What do my feelings tell me about what I'm demanding/ insisting on when I'm thinking about the diploma and how hard it might be? What am I saying MUST or MUST NOT happen?

Jane identifies that she is demanding that she MUST find it easy. She then asks:

What do my feelings tell me about how bad it will be if I do not find it easy when I think the diploma MUST be easy? Are they telling me it will be bad or awful, terrible, horrible, the end of the world?

Jane identifies that it would be bad but not terrible. She then asks herself:

What do my feelings tell me about how difficult it will be if I do not find the course easy when I think it MUST be easy? Are they telling me it will be difficult (hard, tough, frustrating) or unbearable (can't cope, can't stand it)?

Jane identifies that she believes she will not be able to cope if she finds it difficult. She then asks herself:

What do my feelings tell me about what I think of myself if I find it difficult when I think that it MUST be easy? Are they telling me that I failed at finding it easy full stop or are they telling me that I'm a failure (unworthy, useless, loser, bad, weak) because I might find it difficult?

Jane identifies that she believes it would mean that she is stupid.

So Jane's anxiety-provoking belief – when she thinks about applying for the diploma which might turn out to be hard – is:

> I MUST find the diploma easy and not hard. If I find it hard then I won't cope and it would prove that I'm stupid.

Putting it in the ABC model, Jane's first ABC is as follows:

A	B	C
I'm thinking about applying for a diploma in psychology and it might be hard	→ I must find the diploma easy. If I find it hard then I won't cope and it will prove that I'm stupid	→ Anxiety

Jane identifies the 'B' in the second ABC is as follows:

> I MUST know how I will feel if I need to take time away from my family when I'm doing the course. It's awful that I don't know and I cannot stand not knowing how I will feel.

Jane's second ABC looks as follows:

A	B	C
How will I feel if it meant time away from my family	→ I must know how I will feel if I need to take time away from my family. It's awful that I don't know. I can't stand it	→ Anxiety

Jane identifies the 'B' in the third ABC as follows:

> I MUST not take time away from my family during the week to work on my diploma. Doing that would be awful and it would prove I'm a bad mother and wife.

Putting it in the ABC model, Jane's third ABC is as follows:

A	B	C
I'm doing the course and spending too much time away	→ I MUST not take time away from my family during the week. Doing that would be awful and it would prove I'm a bad mother and wife	→ Guilt

---

Exercise

Write down the ABCs you worked on from the last exercise. Take one ABC at a time and ask yourself similar questions, using the following template as a guide:

Q1: What do my feelings of anxiety, anger and so on, tell me about what I'm demanding/insisting? What am I saying MUST or MUST not happen?

Q2: What do my feelings tell me about the badness of not having my demand met? Are they telling me it's bad but not the end of the world or awful, horrible, the end of the world?

Q3: What do my feelings tell me about difficulty of not having my demand met? Are they telling me it will be difficult (hard, tough, frustrating) or unbearable (can't cope, can't stand it, can't tolerate it)?

Q4: What do my feelings tell me about how I judge myself or others as a consequence of not having my demand met? Are they telling me that I failed but that I'm not a failure or are they telling me that I'm a failure (unworthy, useless, loser, rubbish, bad, weak etc.)?

Write down the full unhealthy belief for each of your ABCs. Remember all or some of the four unhealthy beliefs may be present in each of your ABCs. Refer to Jane's examples for guidance.

Put all the unhealthy beliefs under the ABC framework.

GOAL ACHIEVEMENT BELIEFS TO SUPPORT YOUR SMART GOAL

Beliefs that set you up for goal achievement are the healthy versions of the unhealthy sabotaging beliefs. You will recall that healthy beliefs are flexible, consistent with reality, logical and helpful to you.

Healthy beliefs are based on what you want to achieve (internal reality) alongside the acceptance of external reality in order to make it balanced, powerful, logical and helpful. So your healthy beliefs take reality into account while focusing on what is important to you. This means:

Hoping, wanting and striving for the best but accepting and planning for the worst-case scenario by negating the demand.

Accepting that bad things happen with the knowledge that this won't be the worst thing that could happen, that is the end of the world.

Accepting that difficulties arise but that they are bearable as long as you are alive.

Accepting that you are fallible and at times you may not get what you want but you remain a worthwhile human being regardless.

Healthy belief = What you want + Acceptance of reality

The next thing to do is to modify your unhealthy beliefs to include concepts of external reality and truth in them.

Example: Jane's healthy version of her first unhealthy belief

I WANT to find the diploma course easy and not hard BUT I accept there is a chance that I might find it hard.

Another version of this might be:

I hope that I find the diploma course easy and not hard BUT that does not mean I MUST find it easy.

If I find the diploma course hard then that would be difficult but it does not mean that I won't cope.

If I find the diploma course hard then I might be challenged but I will learn to bear it and cope with it.

If I find the diploma course hard it doesn't mean that I am stupid. It just means I am human like everyone else. I remain worthwhile regardless of whether I find the course hard or easy.

Exercise

Write down your unhealthy beliefs.

Take each belief and each element of it and think about why it is unhealthy.

Tip: Why is the 'MUST' unhealthy? Why is catastrophizing badness unhealthy? Why is low frustration tolerance unhealthy? Why is self-, other- or world-damning unhealthy?

Write the healthy version for each of your beliefs. Think about what healthy negative emotions you would feel and what the belief would cause once you have internalized it.

Tip: Healthy negative emotions are, for example, concern instead of anxiety, remorse instead of guilt, annoyance instead of anger.

PERSONALLY PERSUASIVE REASONS – WHAT'S IN IT FOR ME?

This section continues the process of reflection, but this time you will learn to think of personal reasons *in favour of your healthy beliefs* and personal reasons *against your unhealthy beliefs*. This will expand on the theory of the last section. You are now getting into more detail and injecting some energy and passion into your goal. You will be asking yourself:

- What's in it for me?
- What's in it for me in committing to and strengthening my healthy beliefs?
- What's in it for me in keeping my unhealthy beliefs?

This will help strengthen your healthy beliefs and weaken your unhealthy ones. When you can see how you will benefit you are more likely to commit yourself, otherwise you would be unlikely to convince yourself to do it or to focus on it. Your 'what's in it for me' reasons will begin to motivate you towards your goal. It makes sense in so many different areas of life. Think of something that you look forward to, like going on a holiday. If you didn't see any benefits to you personally in going on holiday, the chances of your going become remote.

So what's in it for you in believing that you are a worthwhile but fallible human being? What images does this statement generate in your mind? What feelings does it provoke in you? How does it affect the way that you hold yourself? How would you talk to yourself? What would other people see if you believed it?

You can see how your mind begins to work as you allow yourself to reflect on these questions. You can definitely see there is something in it for you: happiness, confidence and an increased likelihood of success and achievement. That's what is in it for you ultimately.

Your 'what's in it for me' lists will be used in the process of your goal achievement to help you stay focused on what you want. The negative list of 'what's in it for me' in keeping the unhealthy beliefs will be used when you are putting in effort, or when you feel like giving up.

Example

Assume that a man has identified the following unhealthy and healthy belief.

UNHEALTHY BELIEF
People must not judge me negatively when they meet me. If they do, it's awful, unbearable and proves I'm unworthy.

HEALTHY BELIEF

I'd really like it if people did not judge me negatively when they meet me but that does not mean they must not judge me negatively either. If they do, it would be bad but not the end of the world. It would be tough but not unbearable. It would not mean I'm unworthy. I'm fallible, some people will like me and some might not. I remain worthwhile regardless because my worth does not depend on people's negative or positive judgement.

What's in it for me in keeping my unhealthy belief?

- *It makes me feel anxious.*
- *I'm not myself in the company of other people.*
- *I worry about what to say.*
- *I worry about how I'm saying things.*
- *It stops me from engaging.*
- *I'm focused on my feelings and not on the conversation.*
- *It makes my hands shake.*
- *It makes me sweat and go red.*
- *It makes me feel clumsy.*
- *I run out of things to say.*
- *I end up agreeing with everything people say even if I disagree in my head.*
- *It makes me end up talking to people I don't want to talk to.*
- *I end up declining invitations.*
- *It affects my social life badly.*
- *It makes me unhappy.*
- *It makes me withdraw from conversations because I'm thinking about whether they like me or not.*

- *I say things like 'oh, I see', and 'really, that's so funny' even when it isn't.*
- *It makes me feel that I'm bad and not normal.*

What's in it for me in strengthening my healthy belief?

- *I would feel more relaxed and not anxious.*
- *I would be me.*
- *I would enjoy myself more.*
- *I would allow people to know me.*
- *People will probably like me because I'm being me.*
- *I will feel strong and cope if someone does not like me. That's life.*
- *I will express what I think and feel better.*
- *I will agree when I agree with someone.*
- *I will disagree when I disagree with someone.*
- *I will be focused on the conversation and on the people I'm talking to.*
- *I will get a better sense about other people because I won't be in my head all the time.*
- *My hands won't shake.*
- *I will be cool and comfortable.*
- *I will feel that I have a right just like everyone else.*
- *I will like myself.*
- *I will be open and happy.*
- *I will feel more confident in my self.*
- *I will have good conversations and be able to chat up someone I fancy.*
- *I will be relaxed and laugh and joke freely.*

Exercise

Start this exercise by writing down your healthy beliefs, one at a time. Think of all the positive personal benefits to you if you truly believed your healthy statement. What would be in it for you in believing your healthy belief in the short and in the long term? Come up with 10 to 20 positive benefits for each healthy belief.

Write down the unhealthy beliefs, one at a time, and think about what's in it for you in keeping your unhealthy belief. Hopefully, you will see that you derive very little, and definitely nothing that will help you achieve your important goals. This will show all the negative consequences to you personally in keeping these limiting beliefs. Come up with 10 to 20 reasons for each of your unhealthy beliefs.

4
Overcoming Obstacles to Goal Achievement

In this chapter you will learn what happens when you set significant goals and commit to them. You are goal-driven by nature, so setting goals and wanting what is important to you is natural. You also know that most of the time you act in accordance with your beliefs, which trigger your emotions, behaviours and thoughts. If your belief is unhealthy, your emotions, thoughts and behaviours will influence your performance and ultimately the likelihood of achieving your goal. Besides the immediate emotional obstacles that you identified in Chapter 3, other emotional, cognitive, habitual and environmental issues may also get triggered.

Think about what happens when you set a significant goal; for example, going on holiday, buying a car, renting or buying property.

The day before you decide that you want to buy something important, the thought of the item will not have been in your conscious mind. However, as soon as you say to yourself, 'I want to buy X', suddenly your antenna are switched on. You start to become aware of words, pictures, ideas, sounds and emotions related to what you want to buy.

For example, if you decide to rent or buy property, you see 'For Sale' signs everywhere you go. If you think of going on holiday, you take notice of TV adverts for exotic destinations and you become aware of travel agents on your way to work. If you want to buy a vacuum cleaner, you notice them in department stores and shops. If you are thinking about having children, you begin to see pregnant women and children everywhere.

All these things that you become conscious of were there anyway, but as soon as you say 'I want to …' your mind makes you conscious of those things that are related to your goal. Your mind is programmed to strive towards what you want and the things that are important to you so you can attain them and feel happier than you did before. You could say that your mind is your friend, looking after you and helping you towards your goal as long as you are striving towards your desires, as long as you are making choices based on what you want.

However, as soon as any negative, unhealthy 'have to' demands appear, or as soon as any 'end of the world', awful, terrible, catastrophizing, or 'I can't cope', low frustration tolerance beliefs are triggered, it's another story.

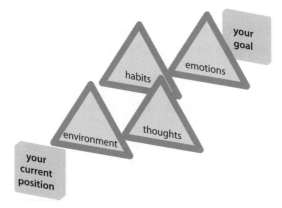

This happens because catastrophizing beliefs and low frustration tolerance beliefs tell your mind that you will, essentially, perish. They provoke unhealthy negative emotions that say 'run and protect yourself from danger'. So when you set and commit yourself to a significant SMART goal, emotional, habitual, cognitive and environmental obstacles are put up like hurdles in a 100-metre race. You now have a choice of getting over the hurdles and running towards the finishing line, or staying behind the hurdles and looking at the finishing line from your current position.

EMOTIONAL OBSTACLES

You already identified unhealthy negative emotions, such as anxiety or guilt, when you set your significant goal.

Unless you change these emotions you will find it difficult to focus on your goal in a positive way. It will feel like someone is holding onto you as you are trying to walk.

You may have an emotion about an emotion too. You may, for example, have an anxiety about your anxiety. This is more commonly known as fear of the fear. You may also have depression about your anxiety, or anger about your anxiety. So, you see, people can disturb themselves about anything.

You will recall that healthy beliefs trigger healthy negative emotions, like concern or annoyance, as opposed to unhealthy emotions, such as anxiety and anger. However, it is also possible that you can create an unhealthy negative emotion about a healthy negative emotion, for example anxiety about healthy nervousness or concern. Negative emotions can feel uncomfortable, you may think it is wrong to feel them or assume that it's an indication that you are not strong enough. However, when you feel healthy nervousness it is absolutely appropriate. When you commit yourself to a goal that you care about, you may feel a healthy negative emotion that will be mixed with a sense of excitement. This healthy but negative emotion is natural. Do not assume that there is something wrong and start worrying about it. If that happens then you may create an unhealthy negative state in response to what was a healthy negative state to begin with.

This could happen at the beginning of goal setting, when you commit to your goal or when you start taking action to achieve your goal. Therefore, you need to watch that you do not create an emotional problem about feeling healthy tension and nervousness.

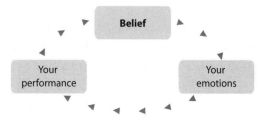

Once you start moving towards your goal, you will open yourself up to what can happen in life. You may be dealing with people, deadlines, making decisions, or considering a number of options. You will open yourself up to things that are both within and outside your control.

Your emotional response will influence your performance and success. And what do you think will be at the heart of your emotional state? It will of course be your beliefs, whether healthy or unhealthy.

Example

Jonathan is a 45-year-old man who has been self-employed for a year after making a goal commitment of starting and running an IT business. However, one of the emotions that Jonathan experiences is anger towards one of his business partners, which started soon after they began working together. His anger is beginning to trouble him, but he is worried that trying to be honest about his emotions might lead him to say things in an inappropriate way, which in turn may affect the business relationship.

THE EMOTIONAL OBSTACLES

1. anger towards one of his business partners; and
2. anxiety about the potential consequences of his anger.

The anger is unhealthy because Jonathan is not acting assertively and expressing how he is feeling about whatever his business partner is or is not doing. Instead he is demonstrating his anger in a passive but aggressive way by not engaging as much with his business partner.

Unless Jonathan resolves these emotional obstacles, he will end up increasing the chances of inappropriate and destructive outbursts.

THE SOLUTION

Jonathan applies the ABC model to identify the unhealthy belief triggering his unhealthy anger. He concludes that he is demanding that his business partner be as organized as he is, and realizes that he labels him as 'inefficient' because of this.

He then rewrites this unhealthy belief as follows:

> I would really like it if my business partner were as organized as me, but he does not HAVE to be. The fact that he is not does not mean he is an inefficient person. He's not perfect but neither am I. He is a worthwhile person regardless of the fact that he is less organized. He definitely has other strengths too.

This process helps Jonathan to gain insight about why he was feeling so angry and he now realizes how to correct what he believed about his partner.

Communication problems

When you begin to experience unhealthy negative emotional obstacles following your commitment to your positive goal, it is important that you begin to find an appropriate and healthy way of dealing with them. Unresolved emotional obstacles will lead you to avoid communicating your feelings effectively. You may then decide to withhold information from others. You may start to relate to others in unhealthy ways, for example you may begin to put them down, gossip behind their backs and generally defocus from solving the problem you are experiencing.

For example, Jonathan recognizes that his feelings of anxiety about potential conflict (if he expresses anger or disagreement) are preventing him from talking to his business partner about being more organized. He realizes that unless he learns to change his feelings of anxiety he will remain unassertive in his new business. Clearly, if Jonathan remains anxious about displaying any annoyance, he will be unable to express his opinions about events at work. This in turn may leave him feeling unhappy, and he might even start withholding information or putting his business partner down in front of other people. The long-term effects of such an unhealthy emotional state are more negative outcomes and communication problems.

Jonathan writes his healthy belief as follows:

> I'd really like not to end up with detrimental business problems when I talk to my partner about being more organized, but I accept that such a possibility exists. If it happens, it would be really bad but it won't be a world disaster; it would be very unfortunate and difficult but I would be able to cope and deal with it somehow.

As you can see, the first thing is that this belief frees Jonathan to talk to his business partner. He is no longer in that state of anxiety. Working on his first anger-provoking belief ensures that Jonathan will be able to express his feelings and thoughts in an appropriate way. His first healthy belief will help him be as appropriate as he can be. His second healthy belief will allow him to do it.

Exercise

Reflect on the emotional obstacles you became aware of when you committed yourself to your significant goal, for example, anxiety, anger, guilt, envy.

Identify the unhealthy belief for each emotional obstacle. Ask yourself about the consequences of not having your demand met. Do your feelings tell you it would be awful, unbearable or that you are unworthy?

Write down the healthy versions of your unhealthy emotional obstacles.

Example: I want to xyz but I don't have to xyz. If I don't it would be bad but not terrible, difficult or unbearable; I'm not unworthy. I'm fallible and my worth does not depend on anything. It's inside me.

Write the 'what's in it for me' reasons for focusing on the healthy belief and the 'what's in it for me' reasons for focusing your energy on the unhealthy beliefs that are causing your emotional obstacles.

HABITUAL AND BEHAVIOURAL OBSTACLES

Habitual and behavioural obstacles are hurdles that you can become aware of when you set and commit yourself to a significant goal.

Habits are learned behaviours and actions that have been repeated so many times that they become automatic and feel effortless. They are stored in the subconscious part of the mind, so you don't consciously think about them, you just do them because you are so used to them.

Habits can be good, bad or neutral

Good habits include knowing what your name is or the names of your friends and colleagues, driving your car well or cycling. If your brain did not have this ability to learn and store what you have learned, you would always have to think about how to do things. When you first start taking driving lessons, for example, you are conscious of how bad you are at driving and everything feels like an effort. You concentrate hard and try to remember what your driving instructor is telling you: mirror, check, signal, check, manoeuvre, check. You are very conscious of everything you are doing. In other words, you are consciously incompetent.

As you keep practising and showing up for your driving lessons, you begin to feel more capable. You are still consciously learning and extremely aware of your surroundings and other cars on the road. You are consciously putting into practice what you are learning, but it still does not feel effortless. You are now consciously competent.

Then you pass your driving test and are driving on your own to work and to the supermarket. One day you realize that you have not consciously thought: mirror, signal, manoeuvre. In fact you have been listening to the radio and smiling or singing to yourself. Now, you are unconsciously competent. Driving has now become a habit.

You may also unconsciously begin to believe that you are the best driver ever and start racing others on the road. You are now speedily moving into becoming unconsciously incompetent as a driver. If something unfortunate happens, you start the whole process of re-evaluating your skills and reflecting on what you have learned over again.

It is easy to see how habits can develop. The same process can happen with something negative, like being late for appointments, eating everything on your plate even when you are full, or driving everywhere, even to the corner shop. When you commit yourself to a significant goal, you may become aware of habits that stand between you and your goal. Will you keep the habit or the goal? If your goal is important then you keep the goal and learn a new habit by stopping the one that is causing the obstacle.

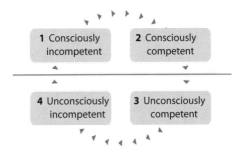

Example

Maggie recently decided to lose 10 pounds in weight. She is doing well with both her food intake and the exercising, but the weight is not coming off as quickly as she had planned. She realizes that she has a social drinking habit that has become an obstacle; as soon as she is with friends she automatically says yes to offers of drinks and partying. The next day she remembers that she really needs to take more control and stick to her goal. It is only then that she becomes aware of letting go of her goal.

THE HABITUAL OBSTACLE

Maggie's habit of social drinking a few times a week is working against her goal of weight loss. She automatically and unconsciously falls into the same behaviour of accepting drinks without consciously thinking about what she is doing or keeping her goal in mind. This in turn maintains the habit and she loses sight of her goal. She will find it difficult to lose the extra 10 pounds without changing or modifying her social drinking habit.

THE SOLUTION

Maggie decides to keep her goal in mind and have only a couple of drinks when she goes out. However, she notices that she begins to feel tension in her body when she starts to say 'no' and usually ends up having more drinks.

She asks herself what her feelings are telling her about her demands when she is saying no to alcohol. She understands that she is demanding that she MUST have the drink right now and that she can't stand not having one like everyone else. In that moment she is also letting go of her significant goal of losing weight.

She considers this unhealthy belief and she rewrites it as follows:

> I would like to have a drink right now but I don't have to. The fact that I'm choosing not to have one is uncomfortable but I can stand not having a drink. I want to lose the 10 pounds.

This new belief is helpful and constructive. It reminds Maggie that it is her choice to reduce her drinking and that she is doing it because she wants to achieve her desired goal. She helps herself to feel more motivated about her choice by writing down a list of 'what's in it for me' in adopting the healthy belief as opposed to the unhealthy demand.

The example illustrates that when you start changing a habit you will feel tension in your body because you are giving up one thing that feels 'natural' and automatic in favour of something new that you are not used to. Unless you then work on the belief that is causing the tension and write its healthy version, the chances of giving in to the habitual obstacle increase.

Exercise

Reflect on the habits that you feel will or have become an obstacle to your goal achievement, for example lying down in front of the TV instead of writing letters to potential customers.

Start by changing the habits and notice what you feel in your body. If you find that you have been giving in to your old habits, identify the emotion and tension you felt when you tried to change the habit.

Identify what your emotions were telling you about what you were demanding when you started to change the habit, for example: 'I must watch TV and feel comfortable'.

Become aware of what your feelings were telling you when you stopped the habit. Did they tell you it's terrible or that you can't stand not doing the habitual thing?

Write the healthy version of the unhealthy habitual belief.

Write a list of 'what's in it for me' in focusing on the healthy belief, and 'what's in it for me' in keeping the unhealthy habitual belief in terms of your goal achievement.

COGNITIVE OBSTACLES

Cognitive obstacles are particularly unhelpful attitudes and thoughts that you become aware of when you commit yourself to your goal, or when you are taking action and moving towards your goal.

They get triggered because plans involving your goal may, for example, require you to talk to certain people, put yourself forward for events or make telephone calls.

The attitude you take can either help or hinder you when you have a goal in mind. Clearly, a negative, judgemental or prejudiced attitude will not set you up for success and may stop you in your pursuit of your goal.

An appropriate attitude is one of the key ingredients in goal achievement. Your attitude towards something or someone can be a function of how you feel about yourself, about other people or about the world. It is related to how you think things should or should not be.

A healthy, optimistic and encouraging attitude comes from a position of strength and acceptance of people and their differences. It comes from being flexible and seeing that other ways and alternative solutions are possible.

When it comes to your goals it is important that you have a strong focus and a flexible, helpful and positive attitude. If you find that you don't then you can always change your attitude and keep your goal.

Example

During a sales team brainstorming session, Stuart is criticized for having a glib attitude. He is told that he behaves in a dismissive way towards certain colleagues and ideas. He is asked to come to the next meeting with a different attitude.

THE COGNITIVE OBSTACLE

A sarcastic or belittling attitude is a smokescreen for low self-esteem. In Stuart's example, his attitude demonstrated his own low self-esteem. In attempting to belittle or dismiss others, he was trying to elevate himself above them, but in a dysfunctional way.

THE SOLUTION

Stuart was not aware of his attitude until it was pointed out to him, so he reflects on this and asks himself why he responded in that way.

He realizes that he felt pangs of anxiety when he did not have creative ideas while others did. He asks himself what his feelings told him about what he was demanding when he did not have creative ideas. He identifies a demand that he absolutely MUST be acknowledged as having the most creative ideas among his colleagues; otherwise, it would mean he was a failure.

Stuart realizes that he was dismissing himself if others did not view him as the most creative during the meeting. His own self-dismissal was triggering his dismissive attitude towards his colleagues.

He reconstructs his belief to its healthy version:

> I'd prefer to have my colleagues acknowledge me as the most creative one, but they absolutely do not have to. If they don't, it doesn't mean I'm a failure. I am worthy but fallible, like everyone.

Stuart began to see that his healthy belief would cause a change in his attitude when he was with his colleagues. His healthy belief would stop his dismissive attitude because he would begin to value rather than dismiss himself.

Exercise

Think about your goal and reflect on your attitude. Write down any negative or ambivalent attitudes you have become aware of.

Identify your unhealthy belief that is supporting your negative attitude. (Work out your demands and any awfulizing, low frustration tolerance and self/other/world-damning beliefs.)

Write the healthy version of your unhealthy beliefs.

Write the 'what's in it for me' reasons to keep the healthy belief and 'what's in it for me' in keeping the unhealthy belief.

How would your healthy belief change your attitude?

Implement the change in attitude!

ENVIRONMENTAL OBSTACLES

Environmental obstacles are associated with your surroundings. They are all the unhelpful factors or hurdles at home or in the office.

How conducive is your environment to achieving your goal? While any long-lasting change comes from a change in your beliefs, it is smart to reflect on how you can make your environment work for you instead of against you when it comes to your goal.

For example, if your goal is weight loss, having a cupboard full of biscuits adds an unnecessary obstacle that increases your chances of giving in to temptation. You need to make your home work with you.

If you live with your partner or family, then their support would be helpful. It is not essential but having the right type of support makes for an easier life. It may be useful to ask for support from your family, but remember it is about asking, not demanding or needing the support.

If you can influence your environment to work for you in terms of your goal, it would make sense to do so. If en -vironmental changes are outside your control you will need to strengthen your tolerance and keep focused on your goal.

Exercise

List the environmental obstacles that are in your control. Begin to change them to make them work with your goal.

List environmental factors outside your control. Identify the healthy attitudes and beliefs that would enable you to remain focused on your goal despite the environmental obstacles.

TOLERATING TENSION AND DISCOMFORT

You know when you are outside your comfort zone because your body naturally gives out signals that you are tense and uncomfortable. The degree of discomfort you feel is triggered by your beliefs and attitude about this. Typically these are low frustration tolerance beliefs about discomfort.

As you know, your beliefs represent what you think of yourself and of your abilities. They function like an automatic pilot. Setting a goal means you want to move from one position to a more satisfactory one. If you wish to lose weight or become confident at giving presentations, your current beliefs may trigger anxiety, tension and thoughts like, 'I'm not good enough' or, 'I can't do it'. They may also trigger you to act in accordance with what you believe and think. You now understand that none of these thoughts are true, but your automatic pilot has been set to create them anyway and as soon as you attempt to change, the automatic pilot switches on, leaving you with your negative thoughts and emotions.

This is not your fault and doesn't mean that you are weak or doing something wrong. It's part of the natural process of change. Your current unhealthy belief is trying to maintain its position because it is strong. If you think and act in accordance with what the belief is telling you, you will continue to strengthen its position even though it is not helpful.

It is easy to understand emotional and physical tension if you think about your currently held unhealthy belief as an energy box that is radiating emotions, negative and limiting thoughts and unhelpful behaviours, as well as physical symptoms.

An unhealthy belief has been reinforced through years of conditioning and repetition. You now know that this belief is unhelpful, but knowing it does not alter what it triggers. Each time you have these negative thoughts, justify them and act as if they are true, their energy is fed back into the belief, causing the energy box to radiate with even more power.

You can choose to adopt a healthy belief instead. The new belief is like a tiny glow that you want to strengthen. For it to start radiating positive feelings, thoughts and behaviours automatically, you need to energize it with constructive, positive, helpful thoughts and behaviours. Only then will you be in a position to feel the positive feelings of confidence. For the process to work, repetition of your healthy belief and helpful behaviours is vital.

The following diagram illustrates this process:

If you attempt to energize the healthy belief so that, in time, it radiates healthy feelings, but at the same time continue to entertain and buy into the unhealthy thoughts and behaviours because you are feeling negative emotions, it's like giving yourself something good with one hand and then throwing it

away with the other. This means healthy emotional change is unlikely to happen.

So how do you make this change?

- You start thinking in a constructive way and challenge the unhealthy negative thoughts.
- You start behaving in a constructive way and stop behaving in an unhealthy way.
- You repeat the above over and over again whilst tolerating the unhealthy negative emotions until . . .
- Your feelings change . . . at last.

When your feelings change after the effort of the above process your healthy belief will be firing on all cylinders. The old unhealthy belief will be starved of its emotional energy.

Think about any change you have already gone through, such as learning a new language, taking driving lessons, learning a new skill. How did you feel at first? Did you feel completely natural or uncomfortably clumsy? When you start putting any new skills into practice you will feel uncomfortable. You might also feel a natural tendency to revert back to the old ways, but if you did that then no change would happen. You would need to keep practising the new way while tolerating the urge to revert back to what feels more like you, until the new way feels natural and automatic.

It's exactly the same with changing beliefs. You are literally changing one habit into another, better habit. So please remember your feelings will change last, when the new belief becomes the new way and the unhealthy belief is the old way and no longer instinctive or automatic.

FOCUSING ON THE GOAL

Your healthy belief is the foundation that supports you in achieving your goal. Your goal is the end result. So it should be exciting when you imagine yourself with your goal achieved.

If you focus on the discomfort of change instead of your goal, you will take your attention off the end result. Your goal needs to be at the front of your mind, not something you remember every now and then.

Think of a 100-metre hurdle runner with his eye on the finish line as he runs towards it, jumping over the hurdles that are in his way. If he focused on the hurdle instead of the finish line, he would crash straight into it and fail.

It's important that you make your goal the focus of your healthy thoughts on a daily basis. The more often you think of the end result, the more likely you will maintain the momentum to do the necessary work to make it happen. When you take your attention off your goal, you let go of what you want to achieve. Taking time to think of your goal only takes a matter of seconds, but it is extremely important.

For example, if your goal is to get your weight down to a particular point, or to slim down to a smaller dress or trouser size, then bringing this image to your mind every day will help. Think of the end result when you wake up, before you have your breakfast, lunch and dinner, and every time you eat something.

You can apply this to any goal. All you need to do is to see the end result daily and as often as you can.

How to tolerate the natural discomfort

So far you've learned that healthy beliefs are the foundation behind goal achievement. You know that the process of change and moving towards your goal feels naturally uncomfortable.

Is there a way to tolerate the natural discomfort you experience when you stretch your comfort zone and start moving towards your goal?

One of the best ways is to use the 'what's in it for me' reasons. You can go over these each day. Coupled with the daily focus on your goal, these will give you the momentum to move through the discomfort of change in a positive and healthy manner. It's like giving yourself a daily shot of positive excitement before you do the work necessary for your goal.

You can now see that what you would have called discomfort, or being out of your comfort zone, can be viewed as excitement and energy which you need. It's the fuel that propels you into action.

To sum up: by focusing on your goal and your healthy belief daily, challenging the unhealthy thoughts, recalling and reciting your 'what's in it for me' reasons, and finally viewing the discomfort of change as natural excitement, you will have the strong mind necessary for your goal achievement. The work and the effort do not feel so daunting now.

Exercise

Go over what you have done so far and write your overall goal, followed by the unhealthy and healthy beliefs. Make a list of 'what's in it for me' underneath your beliefs.

Every day, read and imagine that your goal is achieved.

Recite healthy beliefs and go over your 'what's in it for me' reasons.

Rename any feelings of discomfort you experience as 'natural excitement'.

5
Developing Cognitive Skills Through Your Internal Dialogue

We have thousands of thoughts a day. Our internal dialogue or self-talk is one of the most powerful tools we have.

In this chapter you will learn about the different types of thought you have and how to change them using force and rigour.

The relationship between beliefs and thoughts is shown by this modified diagram from Chapter 2.

This time the relationship is a little more elaborate. You will notice the arrows going in both directions, indicating that beliefs influence what you think, and what you think influences what you believe. Your thoughts influence your performance and your performance may trigger your thoughts. Finally, your performances and beliefs also influence each other.

This interaction can be healthy or unhealthy, helpful or unhelpful. If your belief is healthy, the interaction between your thoughts, performance and belief is also healthy, but if your belief is unhealthy so is the interaction.

INTERNAL DIALOGUE OR SELF-TALK

On any given day, thousands of thoughts go through your mind. Some of these thoughts are called 'internal dialogue' or 'self-talk'. They tend to be the things you say about yourself when you face challenges, obstacles or problems throughout the day. Self-talk usually happens in your head at normal speed. It is just the usual dialogue you have with yourself.

All of us engage in self-talk as part of our cognitive process. What happens when your self-talk is negative and unhelpful? Years of negative, unhelpful self-talk will have an impact. If you continue to feed your mind negative self-talk, eventually you will end up developing an unhealthy belief about yourself or your abilities. This belief will in turn trigger more negative self-talk. The emotional results – and your success – will be hugely influenced by this. Negative self-talk will result in a vicious cycle and become a destructive self-fulfilling prophecy. This means that as your negative self-talk is maintained, your unhealthy beliefs become stronger and your performance and emotions more badly affected. So essentially you end up thinking 'see, I knew I wouldn't be able to do it, that's typical'.

You will recognize negative self-talk from the following expressions:

- *That sounds difficult*
- *I don't think that I can do it*
- *I'm sure I will mess it up*
- *I'm not that good*
- *I'll probably fail*
- *I've always been this way*
- *I give up, it's too much*
- *I can't believe you'd want me on your team*
- *I don't know much about anything*
- *I don't think I'm going to do a good job*
- *I don't think I'll impress anyone*
- *It's just little old me*

If you fill your mind with such thoughts from the moment you wake up until you go to bed, their negativity will impact on you in a fundamental way whenever you think about yourself and your abilities.

If you hold an unhealthy belief, negative self-talk tends to be at its worst when you make a commitment to do something or when there is pressure. It is vital that you are mindful of this when you set goals and begin the process of changing unhealthy irrational beliefs.

NEGATIVE AUTOMATIC THOUGHTS

Negative automatic thoughts (NAT) are the things that you always say to yourself in the same specific situations, such as going to a job interview. They are called 'automatic' because you do not take time to analyse whether they are true or not. You just accept them. They tend to be based on assumptions rather than facts. They are the product of unhealthy beliefs and, if they are not challenged, they reinforce the unhealthy belief.

It is important that you become aware of your negative automatic thoughts and the situations in which they occur, because changing them is another way for you to strengthen your healthy belief, your emotions and results. It is a good idea to identify the unhealthy beliefs that are triggered when you set a goal and the negative automatic thoughts that stem from them. Distracting yourself from them and engaging in sabotaging behaviours will not make them go away.

You will recognize negative automatic thoughts because the unhealthy belief is usually triggered. Negative automatic thoughts also tend to differ from self-talk in that you feel they come into your head faster than ordinary internal dialogue.

YOUR HOT THOUGHTS

Hot thoughts are specific unhealthy beliefs that you become very conscious of, usually in times of intense emotional disturbance. Most unhealthy beliefs tend to be just beyond our conscious awareness, but when the belief is triggered, and particularly when the demand is not being met, you will experience unhealthy negative emotions such as anxiety, anger or rage very intensely. On such occasions your thoughts will be extreme, for example, awfulizing, low frustration tolerance and self- or other-damning patterns may become more pronounced. You will be more aware of thoughts like 'this is terrible', 'I can't bear this' or 'I'm so useless' or 'he's horrible'.

Exercise

Write down your goal, your unhealthy belief and your healthy belief, together with the 'what's in it for me' reasons.

Look at your unhealthy belief and reflect on the type of thoughts it provokes.

Break these thoughts down into:

SELF-TALK

Your usual internal dialogue about the problem, for example 'I'm not into going to the gym'.

NEGATIVE AUTOMATIC THOUGHTS

The rushed thoughts you have when you are in a situation feeling uncomfortable, for example 'exercising is so boring'.

HOT THOUGHTS

For example, 'I can't stand being in the gym a moment longer'.

HOW TO CHANGE INTERNAL DIALOGUE

You already know that habits can be good, bad or neutral. First you start to think about something, then you start to repeat it, and before long it becomes the way you think. It becomes normal and usual. This is the process of habit formation.

Applying the habitual process to self-talk, you will see that it is exactly the same. If you start thinking negatively and do not question the truth, sense or helpfulness of your thoughts but just keep repeating the same old nonsense, then it becomes a habit. Negative self-talk is nothing more than an old bad habit. And you can change it.

The first step in any change process is to identify the problem and then set a goal. You will need to become aware of your negative self-talk by noticing how you describe yourself and your abilities, and what you say about yourself when you are faced with challenges and obstacles. If your general tendency is to say 'I give up', or 'it's too hard', your self-talk is unhelpful to you given your desire to achieve a goal.

After identifying your negative self-talk, think about a more helpful thing to say. For example, if you identify your negative self-talk as 'I give up', the more helpful thought would be 'I'll persist, I don't give up easily'.

Typical examples:

Negative Self-Talk	Helpful Self-Talk
That sounds difficult	*It sounds challenging*
I don't think that I can do it	*I will have a good go*
I'm sure I will mess it up	*I want to do it well*
I'm not that good	*I'm looking forward to learning*
I'll probably fail	*I want to succeed*
I've always been this way	*I'm open to change*
I give up, it's too much	*I'm resilient, I don't give up easily*
I can't believe you'd want me on your team	*Thanks, I'm looking forward to it*
I don't know much about anything	*I'm eager to learn*
I don't think I'm going to do a good job	*I will do my very best*
I don't think I'll impress anyone	*I'm nervous but will go for it*
It's just little old me	*It's me*

These examples are just some of many possible versions of helpful self-talk. Finding your own helpful expressions will make it much easier to integrate them into your thinking.

It is important to remember that your helpful self-talk has to be supported by your healthy belief. If you just work on your self-talk but ignore your healthy belief, the helpful self-talk becomes more difficult to believe. For example, if you take the negative self-talk 'I'll probably fail' and the helpful self-talk 'I want to succeed', you will see that the unhealthy belief 'I must not fail because if I fail it proves I'm a failure' will sabotage your helpful self-talk. So your healthy belief about failure or success becomes: 'I want to succeed but that does not mean I must and if I fail, it does not mean I am a failure. I remain worthwhile but fallible regardless.' Reciting the healthy belief will allow you to integrate the more positive self-talk of 'I want to succeed'.

Essentially you are starting the process of energizing the healthy belief by reciting it and by feeding your mind helpful self-talk while stopping the negative self-talk.

You can see the process more easily in the diagram below:

Recite healthy belief
I want to succeed but it doesn't mean I must. If I don't it doesn't mean I'm a failure. I remain worthwhile but fallible regardless.

Performance and emotions change gradually. Feelings change after effort and consistency.

Repeat helpful self talk
I do my best
I love success
I can handle challenge or failures
My worth is inside me

HOW TO CHANGE NEGATIVE AUTOMATIC THOUGHTS

You can apply the same process to changing your negative automatic thoughts. Begin by identifying the negative automatic thoughts that are the cognitive consequence of your unhealthy belief. Write down more helpful versions that fit with the healthy belief you wish to strengthen in order to achieve your goal. Then replace the negative automatic thoughts as they come into your awareness with their helpful versions and recite your healthy belief. Repeat this process until the helpful thoughts become normal and usual.

Negative automatic thoughts tend to be present in specific situations. This means you will need to be prepared to replace them with their helpful versions there and then, and to recite your healthy belief. Becoming familiar with them in advance will make it easier for you when you are in the situation itself.

The following are some examples of negative automatic thoughts and their helpful counterparts.

Negative Automatic Thoughts	Helpful versions
No one here likes me	*Some people will like me*
She's bored with me	*We have different interests*
	I accept this possibility
I can't think of anything funny to say	*I'll just be me, I'll say something funny when I'm ready*
I can't enjoy myself	*I will learn to enjoy myself sooner or later*

These helpful versions need to be supported by the healthy belief.

HOW TO CHANGE YOUR HOT THOUGHTS

Changing your hot thoughts will yield the best and quickest results. If you are really challenged as a result of your worst scenario happening – for example failing, finding out someone thinks negatively of you, being treated unfairly – and you take control of your thoughts by changing them to their healthy versions in that moment, you will be taking a big step in changing your unhealthy belief. Your healthy belief will help you to deal with the negative situation in the most helpful and constructive way.

The following are some examples of hot thoughts and their healthy counterparts.

Hot thoughts	Healthy versions
I can't stand this	*I can stand this. It's hard but I can stand it*
It's horrible	*It's not horrible. It's bad but not horrible*
I'm such a loser	*I am not a loser. I'm fallible; some people will like me and some won't*

Exercise

Write down your goal and healthy belief together with the 'what's in it for me' reasons.

Look at the negative examples of self-talk, negative automatic thoughts and hot thoughts you worked on in the previous exercise.

Work out their helpful and healthy versions and write them down as follows:

HELPFUL SELF-TALK

For example, 'I'm learning to enjoy going to the gym'.

HELPFUL VERSION OF NEGATIVE AUTOMATIC THOUGHTS

If the negative automatic thought was 'exercising is so boring', the helpful thought could be 'exercising is challenging at the moment but good for my goal'.

HEALTHY VERSION OF HOT THOUGHTS

If the hot thought is 'I can't stand being in the gym for a moment longer', the healthy version would be 'I can definitely stand being in the gym for another half an hour even though it's challenging at the moment'.

Start rehearsing and repeating the healthy versions each time the negative or unhelpful thoughts come into your mind.

Support your helpful thinking by reciting your healthy beliefs when you are challenged.

PAST, PRESENT AND FUTURE EXPRESSIONS

Remember that when you describe yourself, you reinforce positive or negative traits and characteristics. For example, you may automatically say, 'I've always been like this'. In striving for your goals, you need to bring the present and what you are currently doing into your self-talk.

You are usually unaware of how your internal dialogue or self-talk reinforces your healthy or unhealthy beliefs, attitudes and traits. You may carelessly use expressions like, 'yes, that's so me' when you have forgotten something, or you may say, 'I'm always late'. You are allowing these thoughts to continue filtering through your mind, shaping how you think of yourself. If you decide that you want to make a change and achieve your goal, it is important to acknowledge that you are now striving for change and to be mindful of expressions that describe you as you were in the past, with your old habits and attitudes.

Essentially, your self-talk decides that you 'are' or 'are not' a particular way. If you say 'I find going to the gym boring' then you are confirming and reinforcing a past attitude – you are not 'someone who likes the gym'. You may think, 'but that's how I feel about it'. The truth of the matter is that's how you have felt about it up to now. There is a possibility that you may change that thinking if you are open to it, and particularly if you have an important goal to achieve. Expressions based on past conditioning do not take your goal into consideration. If you have a goal to lose weight and going to the gym is one of your weight loss strategies, telling yourself that you are someone who doesn't like the gym will affect your motivation. All you are doing is affirming old thinking, bringing the past into the present and into your future. Instead, you can bring your goal, choice and desires into your mind when you are thinking about the gym.

Changing your self-talk expressions gives you a simple and truthful way of talking about the present. You don't have to lie by telling yourself that you love going to the gym. That would be too far removed from the current truth. But you can say, 'I am choosing to go to the gym and hopefully will learn to enjoy it because I have a goal to achieve'. This new self-talk is a more accurate reflection of what you are now doing and wanting to achieve.

It is equally important to affirm your success and the fact that you are now challenging old traits and behaviours. This is about taking responsibility and acknowledging the helpful changes you are now making. Instead of criticizing yourself, you can give yourself a pat on the back and congratulate yourself on your success or hard work.

You have now learned a way of talking and thinking that is grounded in resiliency and high tolerance of discomfort when you are challenging yourself.

Examples

I used to be someone who hated getting up early; now I choose to get up early to have more time because I want to achieve my goal. In time, getting up early will be easier.

I used to be someone who always said yes; now I'm learning to be more assertive so I'm learning to say no.

I used to be someone who found socializing very hard; now I'm learning to stretch my comfort zone and hopefully I will learn to enjoy it.

I used to be someone who got very anxious; now I'm learning new ways to deal with my feelings and eventually I will feel calm.

I used to be someone who procrastinated a lot; now I'm learning how to beat that habit because I want to be more productive.

Exercise

Write your goal and healthy beliefs down, for example:

Goal: To be confident in social situations in six months' time. Healthy belief: I'd really like people to like me but they don't have to. If they don't, it doesn't mean I'm a failure. I'm worthy but fallible.

Reflect on the self-talk expressions about your traits and habits that are unhelpful to your goal because they fixate you on the past. Write these expressions down, for example: 'I'm always shy in social situations.'

Use the above examples to express your constructive thoughts more truthfully so they can support your goal. For example: 'I used to be shy in social situations. Now I'm learning to be confident by working on my healthy belief.'

FORCE AND RIGOUR

Your thinking needs to be forceful and passionate, like that of those teachers who are very effective at lecturing or presenting and engage your attention and interest. Positively persuasive and memorable teachers are skilled at the following:

- explaining their subject;
- enabling students to personalize the information;
- helping students understand the benefits of what they are learning;
- capturing the attention of their students.

One of the main reasons their subjects appear more interesting and lively is that the information is communicated in a forceful, passionate, energetic and lively manner. Passion and energy help the message to be communicated well, enabling it to sink in and become integrated into the listener's psyche. The same applies when you want to replace your old unhealthy beliefs with the healthy ones.

Healthy beliefs integrate into the psyche more effectively if you rehearse and recite them with force and energy, as opposed to in a lacklustre, half-hearted manner. This way you will believe the healthy beliefs quicker. When this happens your emotions will change accordingly.

You can see how this also applies to your:

- self-talk
- helpful thoughts and
- healthy thoughts.

Think about what happens if you recite your healthy belief in a half-hearted way. For example, read the following in a low, weak voice:

'I am a worthwhile, valuable but fallible person.'

They are just words and reading them in this way conveys no feeling in your body.

Passion, forcefulness and the energy you put behind your words matter when you are trying to trigger an emotional response. Now read the same words, putting all these elements into your voice as you read them:

'I AM A WORTHWHILE, VALUABLE BUT FALLIBLE PERSON.'

You are in the process of changing a habit. This may feel odd at first, but with repetition you will get used to it provided you already know in your head that it is a true, logical and helpful statement. Remember that your feelings will change last. If you did not feel odd when reading it with energy and passion, you will have noticed a stronger positive emotion in your body.

Exercise

Start rehearsing and reciting your healthy beliefs, self-talk, helpful thoughts and healthy thoughts in a forceful and energetic manner at least twice a day and each time the old thoughts creep in.

6
Using Imagination and Visualization

For most of us, the first place to start the process of goal achievement is in the mind.

In this chapter, you will learn different techniques so you can use your imagination, coupled with powerful self-talk, in a vivid and emotive way. Doing this will strengthen your healthy belief when you combine it with your constructive self-talk.

As you start your move towards your goal, you may find that acting in accordance with your healthy belief is overwhelming. It helps to plan and prepare before taking action. Even if you do not find making a change too overwhelming, a great way of engaging your mind in a powerful way is to aim for success but be smart and plan for the worst-case scenario.

This does not mean responding to bad events with a smile and a skip, but experiencing the healthy negative emotions appropriately and then moving on. This is at the core of cognitive behaviour therapy. It is about viewing the glass as half full, but learning to deal with life when the glass is in fact half empty without damaging yourself, so you can eventually see it as being half full again.

In the previous chapter, you learned about the importance of force and rigour in the way you recite and rehearse your healthy belief and in how you use your self-talk and helpful and healthy thoughts. Now you will learn about using your imagination in a vivid way. A powerful imagination is another tool in the resources that enable you to make a change in your beliefs.

Think back to when you experienced a negative event in the past and found yourself stuck. How did you talk to yourself and engage your imagination? It's likely that you were passionate and energetic in talking to yourself negatively. Your imagination was probably powerful and full of emotions. Is it any wonder you felt stuck?

This process can be reversed, using your healthy beliefs and focusing on your goal. You can use passionate intensity and vivid imagination in a different way, for your own good rather than for self sabotage. If you have the ability to sabotage yourself well and truly, then you have the capability of freeing yourself from unhealthy old beliefs. Just take control, challenge your unhealthy beliefs, make a commitment to your SMART goal, use your mind and take appropriate action. And of course you need to repeat it in a consistent manner over and over again.

START WITH YOUR IMAGINATION

There are many ways of using your imagination to strengthen healthy beliefs and weaken unhealthy beliefs. It is more effective to imagine the negative or worst-case scenario first before you move on to positive thinking.

A healthy belief cannot be strengthened without first imagining yourself dealing with the negative scenario in a healthy way and without damning yourself.

Imagining a healthy response to a negative event – healthy belief

Your first task is to vividly imagine yourself responding healthily to not getting what you want.

1. Write down your goal and healthy belief.
2. Sit or lie down.
3. Close your eyes.
4. Breathe in deeply, hold it for three or four seconds and then breathe out gently. Repeat a couple of times.
5. Imagine a scenario or a scene where your healthy desire is not being met. Imagine this as strongly as you can for maximum emotional discomfort. If you are imagining the worst-case scenario then you will feel discomfort. This is natural. It means you have hit the target of your fear.
6. While imagining the worst-case scenario, start reciting your healthy belief forcefully and energetically.
7. Continue to imagine the negative event and recite your healthy belief until you notice a positive change to your emotions.
8. Open your eyes.

What if the feeling of discomfort is overwhelming?

When you imagine the worst-case scenario you may find the feelings of discomfort so overwhelming that you stop the visualization. This only means that the unhealthy belief is very strong. There is a way around this, called the bridging technique, which involves borrowing a more positive feeling from another memory so that you can continue with your initial visualization.

A stronger emotion can override another. If you find that imagining the negative event triggers overwhelming feelings of discomfort, you can use this insight to your advantage. The purpose is to desensitize yourself a little to the imagined negative event.

Essentially you can 'borrow' the feeling of relaxation or positivity from another memory, forming a bridge from one image to another. The positive feelings will mix with the feelings of discomfort attached to the negative image you are imagining.

Triggering a positive feeling and imagining a healthy response to a negative event – healthy belief

1. Write down your goal and healthy belief.
2. Sit or lie down.
3. Close your eyes.
4. Breathe in deeply, hold it for three or four seconds and then breathe out gently. Repeat a couple of times.
5. In your mind, recall a time when you felt very relaxed, or when you had strong positive feelings.
6. Focus on the memory and recall where you were and what was happening.
7. Imagine that memory as if it is happening to you right now.
8. Be aware of the increasing feelings of relaxation or positivity.

9. Imagine these feelings growing stronger.
10. When you are ready, let your mind go blank.
11. Imagine a scenario where your healthy desire is not being met. Imagine this vividly for maximum emotional discomfort. *If you are imagining the worst-case scenario then you will feel discomfort. This is natural. It means you have hit the target of your fear.*
12. While imagining the worst-case scenario, start reciting your healthy belief forcefully and energetically.
13. Continue to imagine the negative event and recite your healthy belief until you notice a positive change in your emotions.
14. Open your eyes.

Practise these techniques daily until your discomfort feels more appropriate and manageable. It is important to do them regularly and they will only take a few minutes. You can go over them at home, on the bus or train, or during your lunch break. The important thing is that you show commitment to achieving your goal by putting in the effort to change your unhealthy beliefs.

USING AUDIO

When it comes to making the process of changing your beliefs varied and interesting, the only limitation is how easy you find it to use your imagination. You may find that visualization doesn't work well for you. Some people have strong visual ability and others find it difficult. If visualization techniques are not your cup of tea, then you can record your healthy beliefs, thoughts and 'what's in it for me' reasons and listen to them instead.

It is very important that you record your healthy beliefs and thoughts in a forceful and energetic manner. The more passion you inject into your recording the more effective you will be at integrating and believing them.

The point here is to make your rehearsal techniques, whether they are imagined or auditory, as memorable and as vivid as possible. This way you will engage your emotions, and the more emotive you make your cognitive techniques, the better.

OTHER AUDIO RECORDINGS

In Chapter 5 you learned how to put together constructive self-talk, and helpful and healthy thoughts. These can also be recorded in a forceful way.

If you like, you can enhance the visualization techniques by first practising them and then listening to the recording of your constructive self-talk, and helpful and healthy thoughts.

You can record instructions for relaxation followed by instructions for the visualization technique, then the audio affirmations and forceful statements. There are many variations – be creative and enjoy creating your own combinations.

The following is a step-by-step guide:

1. Write down your goal and healthy belief.
2. Write down your helpful and constructive self-talk expressions.
3. Write down your helpful thoughts.
4. Write down your healthy thoughts.

5. Record the following:
   * Sit or lie down.
   * Close your eyes now.
   * Breathe in deeply, hold it for three or four seconds and then breathe out slowly and gently.
   * Repeat the breathing exercise five or six times.
   * Recall a time when you felt really relaxed. (Pause for a while.)
   * Now focus on the memory. Recall where you were and what was happening. (Pause for a while.)
   * Imagine yourself in that memory as if it is happening to you right now. Notice the feeling of relaxation. (Pause for a while.)
   * Be aware of the increasing feelings of relaxation. (Pause for a while.)
   * Imagine these feelings growing stronger. (Pause for a while.)
   * Let your mind go blank.
   * Imagine a scenario where your healthy desire is not being met. Imagine this vividly. As soon as you feel uncomfortable recite your healthy belief. (Pause for a while.)
   * Keep reciting your healthy belief more forcefully. (Pause for a while.)
   * Keep reciting your healthy belief until you notice a change in your feelings.
   * Tell yourself that you will ensure your self-talk is powerful and constructive from now on. (Pause for a while.)
   * Repeat your powerful self-talk expressions. (Pause for a while.)
   * Tell yourself that you choose to think in a helpful way in specific situations when you are challenged. (Pause for a while.)
   * Recite your helpful thoughts. (Pause for a while.)
   * Tell yourself that you choose to forcefully replace your negative thoughts when things do not go your way. (Pause for a while.)
   * Recite your healthy thoughts. (Pause for a while.)
   * Recite your healthy belief one last time.
   * Open your eyes.

You can of course open your eyes and read what you have written, and then close your eyes and continue listening to your own instructions. Just read, shut your eyes and begin to imagine vividly.

POSITIVE IMAGERY AFTER YOU HAVE IMAGINED DEALING WITH THE NEGATIVE

So far, the techniques that you have learned are about facing up to the worst-case scenario. This is at the core of changing your unhealthy beliefs. However, once you notice that your feelings are changing – that is you are no longer 'dreading' the negative event – you can move on to positive thinking. Remember to work on the negative event first before you start working towards positive thinking.

Positive thinking means that you start imagining your goal has been achieved. Your goal is about your desire but it needs to be supported by your healthy, realistic belief. Now you can imagine that you have achieved your desire and goal.

Two futures – positive visualization technique

This technique involves imagining yourself dealing with not getting what you want in a powerful and healthy way and then imagining yourself getting what you want. These two images are both supported by your healthy belief.

1. Write down your goal and healthy belief.
2. Sit or lie down.
3. Close your eyes.

4. Breathe in deeply and hold it for three or four seconds and then breathe out gently. Repeat this five or six times.
5. Recite your healthy belief in a forceful and energetic manner. You can do this either silently or out loud.
6. Imagine the negative event of your healthy belief but imagine yourself responding in a healthy and helpful manner.
7. Recite your healthy belief again.
8. Imagine your goal achieved.
9. Open your eyes.

You can add other techniques; for example, you can start with the relaxation or positive feelings technique. You can also record the instructions for this technique, then just lie down, listen and participate in your imagination.

MORE ON SELF-TALK

You have already learned about the significance of your self-talk or internal dialogue. Imagining yourself striving and achieving your goal needs to be combined with constructive and helpful thinking. There is little point in taking time to imagine yourself dealing with the negative event and imagining yourself with your goal achieved if you revert to old ways of thinking for the rest of the day.

Sometimes it's very easy to read about different techniques and then to forget about them. It's important to put what you are reading into practice, otherwise all you will have is knowledge and insight without a change in your emotions. It is important that you take control of your self-talk and change it to ensure it is constructive and helpful to you.

Your self-talk needs to help you to remain open-minded, creative and focused on your goal.

Be aware that you will feel some discomfort when you make the effort to practise your visualization techniques. This is natural. Take care to ensure that your internal dialogue reflects this natural state and make it positive, hopeful and constructive.

You have already planned your helpful self-talk expressions relating to your belief. Remember that changing self-talk is like changing an old habit and you will need to:

- Understand the problem of negative self-talk.
- Understand what the positive, powerful and constructive self-talk is all about.
- Make a commitment to yourself to change the old negative self-talk habit.
- Remind yourself of this goal daily.
- Stop the negative self-talk and immediately change it to its helpful and positive version.

If you follow these steps you will become very aware of your self-talk and become more and more proficient at changing it.

Keep reminding yourself of your commitment to healthier self-talk. One way is to write down your commitment in the form of an affirmation, in other words a statement of your new position on something, or how you want to be in the future, as if it has already happened.

Structuring an affirmation

An affirmation describes how you wish to be with a positive benefit, written as if it has already happened. The following guidelines will help you to write your affirmation:

- *Use first person:* 'I'.
- *Use present tense:* 'I am' instead of 'I will'.

- *Be positive:* 'I am calm because my self-talk is constructive' instead of 'I am not anxious because my self-talk is constructive'.
- *Be realistic:* don't use the words 'always' or 'never'.
- *Make it emotive:* use powerful words that trigger positive emotions for you, for example, 'I am achieving because my self-talk is powerful and helpful'.

Reflective exercise

As with most things in life, your affirmation about your self-talk needs to include something that will motivate you, in the same way as your 'what's in it for me' reasons. Think about why positive and powerful self-talk is of benefit to you. Would it help you to feel more confident? Would it encourage you to become more goal striving? Would it help you to take more risks and feel less fearful? What would it do for you?

Take a couple of minutes to write down your answers to the above questions.

Write your own self-talk affirmation using the guidelines above.

How to use your self-talk affirmation

Once you have written your self-talk affirmation (for example, 'I feel confident because my self-talk is positive and helpful'), the next step is to start repeating it mentally, as often as you can, every day. You have learned about reciting your healthy beliefs and helpful and healthy thoughts forcefully and energetically. You've learned about the value of visualization in integrating the healthy belief. The same rules apply to affirmations about your self-talk.

Rehearsing your self-talk affirmation needs to be forceful, energetic and, where possible, vivid. For example, you can write your affirmation and save it as a computer screen saver so it flashes in front of you as you work. You can write it on a big sheet of coloured paper and have it next to your bed so that you see it immediately when you wake up. You can stick it on your fridge so that you see another vivid reminder every time you open it. In your car, you can stick it on the mirror or on the dashboard.

You can also use metaphoric imagery to remind yourself of your self-talk commitment. For example, you might imagine yourself in a gym practising pull-ups over a bar and on that bar are the words 'self-talk' – you could use such words as powerful or uplifting or strong. This is a really useful, vivid and highly emotive way of working.

Read the following affirmation:

> I find it easy to keep my internal dialogue positive and helpful.

Take a moment and think about the metaphoric image it conjures up in your mind.

Bring this image to mind each time you recite and rehearse your self-talk, helping to integrate your new way of thinking. Your self-talk influences and reinforces your belief and performance so it is important for you to take control of it and make it work for the benefit of your goal.

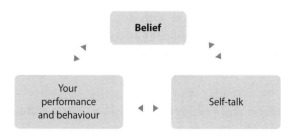

FUTURE IMAGE

All of your constructive imagery work on integrating healthy beliefs is future-based, meaning that you are imagining it as if it has already happened. This helps you to shift to your new belief about what you can do – provided, of course, you have already identified your unhealthy belief and accepted the notion that the possibility of not getting what you want exists, that is you are working in accordance with your healthy belief.

When you begin to imagine yourself doing something proactive and constructive, sooner or later you will begin to accept that you can in fact do it. So imagining yourself as you want to be as if it has already happened strengthens your belief in your own abilities. You will begin to allow for the possibility that you can do it. You will start to feel a sense of motivation and eagerness to get on with it. Remember that as obstacles are identified, you work to overcome them without compromising your healthy goal. This means you continue to imagine yourself with your goal achieved as you deal with the obstacles in an appropriate way.

Once you begin to integrate the possibility that you can do something which previously felt too overwhelming, and once your self-talk is congruent with this, you can reach a plateau. This means you now believe that you can do what you want to do. You are acknowledging your potential. If you are at this stage but still finding it difficult to put your plan into action, you can step up a gear in your cognitive skills and start thinking and talking to yourself as if you have achieved your goal. This means you are now talking in accordance with your goal-achieving self. Start using expressions that demonstrate your commitment rather than your potential.

For example:

- *'I am working towards my goal.'*
- *'I am dealing with challenges and obstacles.'*
- *'I am overcoming my fears.'*
- *'In the past I used expressions like "I can"; now I say "I am".'*

So at this stage you stop the self-talk expressions that are based on your potential 'I can' or 'I will at some point'. This is simply because you are now beyond that point. You now know that you have the potential, and your thoughts need to generate and trigger the natural feeling of discomfort and excitement of commitment. As you know, in order to drive faster, you shift a gear. This is your shift in gear, cognitively speaking.

REPETITION

Repetition is one of the significant parts of the change process. Do it again and again and again and again. All your usual, automatic ways of functioning have become effortless because you have repeated them.

Your unhealthy beliefs and negative self-images only became believable because you entertained them in your mind and thought about them with force and passion. You repeated them energetically. You imagined them vividly.

To shift to the healthy side and to strengthen your healthy beliefs, to change your self-talk, to move towards your goal, requires you to repeat them in a forceful, energetic and vivid way. You were an expert at doing that on the unhealthy, negative side. All you have to do is apply the same degree of commitment and repetition to your goal and healthy beliefs. In time you will experience a shift in your beliefs and self-image.

Everything in your life that you are confident about has gone through the same process. You repeated constructive thoughts and imagined powerful, positive and strong images about yourself and acted accordingly. Emotive repetition has been at the core of it all.

You have repeated the negative and the positive in the past, not just once or twice but many, many times. You have been like a passionate broken record. Now you need to apply the same passion to your new beliefs, thoughts and goals. You can keep these concepts and beliefs alive by imagining them, rehearsing them and talking about them to yourself. Make sure you repeat them by using diagrams, stickers, audio machines and anything that helps trigger your memory. By committing to the repetition, you will be making a commitment to yourself.

7
Developing Resiliency

You've learned that in order to shift and change your beliefs you need to tolerate the discomfort of change. Re-naming these feelings as natural discomfort and excitement may help you accept this state more easily and so not give up. Effectively, you are putting a positive spin on this feeling of discomfort.

While you are tolerating this natural state of discomfort, you also need to keep focusing on your goal and deal with any challenges that spring up along the way. You can do this by changing your unhealthy beliefs and the different types of thought they trigger, replacing them with their healthy versions. One of the things you can be sure of in this whole process is feeling and experiencing the discomfort and challenge of change. Using the cognitive skills you have learned so far, you can develop resiliency to help you bounce back from any setbacks while learning from the challenges they present.

Your mind is a reservoir of experiences, memories, learning and resources that you can put to good use to help you tolerate your emotions and remain focused on your goal. You will learn a specific, structured approach to thinking called 'disputing' to help you respond to challenges and strengthen your resiliency. You can use disputing skills whenever you experience emotional challenges.

You may experience a number of challenges when you want to achieve something. Some are within your control and some are not. Whether or not these experiences are within your control, it will always come down to how you are feeling about them and if those feelings are unhealthily negative.

CHALLENGES WITHIN YOUR CONTROL

Your own beliefs

On the whole your beliefs, healthy or unhealthy, are now up to you. Everyone is shaped by their upbringing, how they are nurtured and the influence of people in their lives when growing up. As a child, you may have been persuaded into your beliefs but this does not mean you are stuck with them forever, especially if they are at the heart of your problems now. You can change them.

Even if someone has been well nurtured, this is no guarantee that they will grow up with healthy beliefs about everything. Everyone has unhealthy beliefs. As an adult, you are responsible for how you wish to live. If you wish to live in accordance with unhelpful beliefs about yourself, your past, your parents, the world, then you need to accept that you choose to live this way. Your unhealthy beliefs will be triggering your emotions, behaviour, thoughts and symptoms.

You may not have had a choice as a child, but now you can make a better choice for yourself. It may not be easy, but it is possible to change your unhealthy beliefs and learn to live more happily.

These beliefs may be about:

- love
- rejection
- failure
- making mistakes
- being perfect
- talking in public
- blushing
- confrontation
- being thin or fat, tall or short
- getting on a train, plane or car
- being on your own
- getting married
- having children
- death
- loss
- acceptance
- trauma and tragedy
- control
- certainty
- to name but a few.

Your own feelings (on the whole)

There are some psychological and medical conditions, illnesses and injuries that can cause problems with feelings, but on the whole it's up to you. If you can accept that generally speaking we are responsible for how we feel and act in the here and now, you can change these by changing your unhealthy beliefs.

The intensity of your disturbed feelings depends on how forcefully you hold dogmatic and demanding beliefs. The intensity of your healthy but negative feelings depend on how strongly you hold your desire or preference belief.

The stronger your 'must' belief, the more intense unhealthy negative feelings, like anxiety, will be. The stronger your 'I want but I don't have to' belief, the stronger your healthy negative emotions, like concern, will be.

Both types of feelings can be extremely uncomfortable so you need to develop resiliency and strength to tolerate the discomfort and not give up.

Your own behaviour and performance

If any problem behaviour is beyond your capability to alter at the moment and is affecting you or someone in your family, you may need to seek medical or therapeutic help. If, however, you feel that with understanding and guidance you can create the necessary change on your own, then remember that behaviour is a consequence of beliefs, we are responsible for how we behave.

Your performance will be affected when you face difficulties and challenges. For example, if you have an interview to go to but receive some tragic news, your performance would be affected. It would be totally understandable if you chose to postpone your interview.

Like the process of changing your thoughts and feelings, changing your behaviour can be uncomfortable. You need to develop resiliency and strength to tolerate this feeling in order to achieve your desired goal.

Your thoughts

On the whole, the thoughts that are involved in your emotions are provoked by your beliefs. In the previous chapters you learned how to challenge and change different types of thought. Thinking is habitual and, as you know, changing any habit or pattern is uncomfortable, so developing resiliency and strength will help you to tolerate any discomfort.

CHALLENGES OUTSIDE YOUR CONTROL

Other people

How other people feel and behave is outside your control. You cannot control what other people say, do or feel. You are responsible for your behaviour and how you talk to others and they are responsible for their response and their behaviour towards you. You can, however, learn to influence other people by first looking at your own behaviour and your own communication skills.

Some people behave passively in the face of aggressive behaviours, and this passivity is their responsibility. They may tolerate aggressive behaviour for their own reasons, for example anxiety and fear or simply pragmatism. It is their own belief systems that influence their behaviour.

No matter how skilled you are at communication, other people are outside your control. Accepting that other people are outside your control and that they can do, say and think as they wish can be challenging and uncomfortable. Developing resiliency and strength will help you to tolerate this feeling.

Certainty in everything

You may have beliefs that demand that you be certain before you can allow yourself to make a change or do something new. Unhealthy beliefs about certainty, just like unhealthy beliefs about control, are very common. They are also very unhelpful to you.

Unhealthy beliefs about certainty – which is different from likelihood – need to be changed because they will stand between you and your goal. It's important to accept that risk is part of life. There is always a risk (or chance) that something can go wrong, for you or for anyone. You cannot totally eliminate risk in order to have absolute certainty that everything will work as you want it to. If that is your goal, you will be waiting a long time and not living your life freely. You will know if you have unhealthy beliefs about uncertainty because they trigger you to feel anxiety and behave in an avoidant way. You can minimize risk and increase certainty to a point where you feel able to act, which will vary depending on how risk averse you are. In these situations you need to consider the consequences, but remember the saying 'no risk, no reward'.

Changing beliefs that demand certainty and no risk can feel uncomfortable, and you need to develop resiliency and strength to tolerate this feeling.

RESOURCES FOR RESILIENCY

Meta emotions

It is very important to develop resiliency and strength to help you tolerate the feelings of discomfort so that you can make a change. You can disturb yourself about any feelings you may have, whether they are healthily or unhealthily negative.

This feeling about another feeling is called a meta emotion. It's effectively having a problem about a problem. Meta emotions play a significant role in resiliency.

If you have a problem about uncomfortable emotions or about discomfort then you will have an unhealthy belief about discomfort. It means you will be making a demand not to feel uncomfortable or for change to feel comfortable.

Typical unhealthy beliefs about discomfort will be as follows:

- I must feel comfortable when I start something new because I cannot stand feeling uncomfortable; feeling uncomfortable is horrible.
- I must not feel any discomfort when I am doing anything because I cannot tolerate feeling discomfort – it's awful.
- I must feel totally calm and relaxed when I do anything; feeling nervous or anything apart from calm is horrible and I cannot cope.
- I must feel confident when I decide to do something because I cannot bear feeling unconfident – it's awful.
- I must feel confident when I start anything new because if I don't it proves I'm useless.
- I must feel confident when I strive for my goals because if I don't it means I'm useless.
- I must not feel any negative emotions when I do anything related to my goals because if I do it's unbearable.

All the above beliefs are dependent on feeling comfortable, and you know that any change will naturally feel uncomfortable. The problem with demanding change to be a comfortable process is that it only increases your vulnerability to disturbance and lowers your tolerance of discomfort. You will be oversensitive in relation to feelings of discomfort, which is quite the opposite of resilience.

Examples of healthy beliefs about comfort or discomfort

- *I want to feel comfortable when I start something new, but it doesn't mean I must feel comfortable, because I can stand feeling uncomfortable even if I don't like it. Feeling uncomfortable is not horrible, it's just bad.*
- *I do not want to feel any discomfort when I am doing anything but I accept that I might. I can tolerate feeling discomfort even if it's hard; discomfort is bad but not awful.*
- *I'd like to feel totally calm and relaxed when I do anything but I accept that I might not. Feeling nervous or anything apart from calm is not horrible, it's just bad and I can cope with it even if I don't like it.*
- *I'd like to feel confident when I decide to do something but it doesn't mean that I must feel confident. I can bear feeling unconfident even if it's hard at first. Feeling unconfident is bad but not awful.*
- *I'd like to feel confident when I start anything new but I accept that I might not. Feeling unconfident does not mean I'm useless. I'm fallible and my worth does not depend on whether I feel confident or not.*
- *I want to feel confident when I strive for my goals but I accept that I might not. It doesn't mean I'm useless. I'm fallible and I remain worthy whether I feel confident or not.*
- *I'd really like to not feel any negative emotions when I do anything related to my goals but I accept that I might. Feeling negative emotions can be challenging but I can bear that and cope with it.*

Having healthy beliefs about feelings of comfort and discomfort will increase resiliency and strength. They help you understand that change is naturally uncomfortable. Discomfort shouldn't be avoided or thought of as a sign that you are doing something wrong. It is uncomfortable when you start to change your beliefs, thoughts and behaviour and start taking action, but this is good because it means you are going through the process of change and being resilient. However, if you begin to find the level of discomfort too much, it means you have an unhealthy belief about it and you need to apply the CBT process to change it.

Use imagery work if you find it helpful

Imagine that you are getting on with taking action even though you feel uncomfortable. This will help prepare you for tolerating the discomfort when you come to face your challenges.

Challenges are temporary

If you think back to any difficulties or challenges you have experienced, you will find that most of them have been temporary. When you experience such a challenge it 'feels' like it will last forever and you just want it to be over. This is understandable because you experience a lot of discomfort. You now know, however, that if you seek comfort in all things, you won't do much and then even that begins to trigger discomfort.

You have the ability to learn from difficult experiences, setbacks and failures. You can learn to improve your skills and adopt healthy beliefs, so challenges are temporary because you can do something constructive about them. You can get up and have another go and this time you have learnt that:

- A challenge or a setback is not the end of the world, it's just bad.
- A challenge or setback is hard and frustrating, but not unbearable.

- You remain a worthy but fallible person who can learn to do it better the next time.
- A setback or a challenge is a temporary hurdle.

Metaphoric imagery about resiliency

Emotive imagery that's relevant to the healthy belief and goal is not only effective in promoting change but also helps your motivation. Imagery work can be either specific and realistic or metaphoric. The important thing is that the metaphor is relevant to your personal change and growth.

Metaphors have been part of meaningful human communication and storytelling for thousands of years. Sometimes a metaphor encapsulates an explanation in a very vivid and profound way. Children's stories are full of metaphors because they can be understood in childhood. For example, you can metaphorically describe the concept of 'hope' by saying that 'spring always follows winter'. You can imagine yourself in the winter when the weather is cold and wet, but sooner or later spring arrives and you see subtle bursts of colour, budding plants and sunnier days.

Metaphors need to appeal to you so that you can use them emotively and vividly. A metaphor with imagery needs to trigger a positive emotional response in you for maximum effectiveness. Start thinking how you can depict resiliency in a metaphoric way with you at the centre of it. What images and pictures does the word 'resiliency' conjure up in your mind? What would you be doing in this metaphoric image of resiliency? The important thing is that it's meaningful to you and triggers a strong, positive emotion.

There are many ways that you can depict resiliency in a metaphoric image, some of which are suggested below.

Mountain metaphor

For example, you can imagine that you are climbing a mountain because at the top is something that you want or an object that you treasure. You start at the bottom, climbing some way and then slipping back, climbing some more and slipping back. You keep imagining yourself getting up and starting to climb again. You are sweating and out of breath from the effort, but you keep on, and you keep climbing back after each slip. You imagine that you are focused on getting to the top of the mountain and then, finally, you imagine yourself there, smiling and raising your hands up to the sky.

Boulder metaphor

This time, you are pushing a big, heavy boulder up a hill. Don't ask why, it's a metaphor. You imagine falling down and slipping back all the way to the beginning, getting back up again and starting to push the boulder back up the hill. You repeat the image of slipping and starting again until you eventually imagine yourself making the final push, the boulder is on top of the hill and you are sitting on top of it looking very pleased with yourself.

100-metre hurdle metaphor

Or you can imagine that you are running a 100-metre hurdle. You imagine yourself falling down from crashing into the hurdles and tripping, getting up and going towards the next hurdle. You fall at some but get up and jump over others, with a determined look on your face, focused on getting to the end. Finally you imagine breaking through the finish line with your hands up, a winner.

Think of your own metaphoric image for resiliency and imagine overcoming setbacks whilst remaining focused on your goal.

Positive imagery technique for developing resiliency

You can use imagery to trigger positive emotions that enable you to de-sensitize any overwhelming feelings of discomfort you may have during the change process or when you experience a setback. Using positive imagery can help you to cope by triggering positive feelings to counteract the discomfort. Both the overwhelming and the positive emotions are represented by different images. Both images are triggered by imagining them at the same time, or by imagining them fusing together. This technique should be used when you rehearse the healthy belief about discomfort; recite your healthy belief about discomfort or resiliency, and then imagine fusing the image associated with the overwhelming feeling of discomfort to the image associated with positivity.

1. Write down your goal and healthy belief about resiliency.
2. Sit or lie down.
3. Close your eyes.
4. Breathe in deeply, hold it for three or four seconds and then breathe out gently. Repeat this five or six times.
5. Imagine that you are drifting off to your own favourite place of relaxation where you feel most at peace. This could be a place you know well, a place you have read about or a place you have dreamt of.
6. Imagine yourself at your favourite place and let the feelings of relaxation happen naturally.
7. Create an image of the overwhelming feelings of discomfort you experience and put it to one side of your mind.

8. Recall a time when you have felt very relaxed, calm and at peace. Imagine that this is happening to you right now. Let the feelings of calm and relaxation flow through your body as you visualize this memory.

9. When you feel very relaxed, recall the image that represented the overwhelming feelings of discomfort.

10. Recite your healthy belief about resiliency.

11. Let the image that represented the overwhelming feelings of discomfort drift to the back of your mind.

12. Remember a time when you felt confident and in control. It doesn't matter how long ago it was; just recall the memory, where you were at that time and what was happening.

13. Imagine yourself in this memory of confidence and control as if it is happening to you right now.

14. Let the feelings of confidence and control grow.

15. When these positive feelings are vivid, recall the image that represented the overwhelming feelings of discomfort.

16. Recite your healthy belief about resiliency.

17. Put the image that represented the overwhelming feelings of discomfort to one side of your mind.

18. Recall a memory when you felt very amused and laughed a lot.

19. Imagine yourself in that funny memory and recall who was there and what happened.

20. Imagine yourself in that funny memory as if it is happening to you right now.

21. Let the feelings of laughter grow inside you.

22. When you feel amused, bring to the forefront of your mind the image that represented the feelings of discomfort.

23. Recite your healthy belief about resiliency.

24. Let your mind go blank and then imagine yourself back in your favourite place of relaxation.

25. Recite your healthy belief about resiliency and imagine yourself dealing with the setback, focused on your goal and actions.
26. Tell yourself that you will now open your eyes and that you will be back in the present, feeling good and whole.
27. Open your eyes.

You can also record these instructions on an audio machine and follow them by listening and imagining.

The above technique is really about desensitizing you to unhealthy meta emotions. If you are anxious about discomfort, for example, this technique will help you overcome your anxiety about uncomfortable feelings and help you to increase your tolerance. For maximum effectiveness, use it while rehearsing your healthy belief about discomfort.

COGNITIVE EMOTIVE TRIGGERS

Cognitive emotive triggers are words or statements that you can use to trigger positive feelings whenever you experience an emotional challenge or setback. When this happens, some form of 'sticking plaster' technique may come in handy, like a cognitive 'pick me up'.

It is important to remember that these techniques are a short-term measure, and any long-term change needs to come from working on your beliefs. Cognitive emotive triggers can take the sting out of emotional challenges and setbacks that you face in the short term.

Cognitive emotive triggers are about provoking a positive feeling when you encounter a setback. You will not feel the full intensity of the positive emotion because you will be feeling discomfort from the setback and challenge. At the same time, you can expect the negative emotion to feel less intense. Your ability to tolerate the setback and to bounce back will increase or, to put it another way, if you mix a bowl of hot water and a bowl of cold water, you have warm water.

You can learn how to do this by associating your positive feelings with a word or/and an image. You start by triggering your positive emotions and then associate the emotional state to the word and the image you have chosen. You repeat this process a few times to reinforce the association. Once you have set the cognitive emotive trigger, all you need to do whenever you feel an emotional challenge, or experience a setback, is to repeat your trigger word and quickly flash the image in your mind. This triggers the emotion that you have associated with the word and the picture.

How would you want to feel if you were to experience a setback? The best 'sticking plasters' are feelings of calmness and confidence. You then think of a picture or image to go with feelings of calmness and confidence. You can also think of a colour that for you relates to calmness and confidence. Then finally you think of a word or statement that is meaningful to you. You can think 'resilient and strong', or you can think 'resilient and calm', whatever words or expressions are most suitable for you. Once you have thought of these three things, words, image and feeling, you can follow the instructions below:

1. Sit or lie down.
2. Close your eyes.

3. Breathe in deeply and hold it for three or four seconds and then breathe out gently. Repeat this five or six times.
4. Recall a time when you felt calm and confident.
5. Imagine yourself in that time when you had feelings of calm and confidence.
6. Allow these feelings of calm and confidence to grow inside you until you feel them.
7. Keep the feelings of calm and confidence and intensify them in your own way.
8. Open and close your eyes quickly.
9. Imagine or visualize your new picture or colour that depicts calmness and confidence and repeat your trigger word or statement, for example 'I'm resilient'.
10. Repeat your trigger word or statement four or five times in a forceful and energetic way.
11. When your feeling of calmness and confidence decreases, open your eyes.
12. Repeat from 1 to 11 twice more.

Now you have a 'sticking plaster' to use whenever you experience an emotional challenge or setback, but please remember that this is a quick, short-term technique. If you feel stuck in the emotional challenge or setback, it means you have an unhealthy belief and you then need to do the more in-depth work of changing it, as outlined in Chapters 3 and 4.

Disputing

Disputing is a cognitive skill that involves questioning both your unhealthy and healthy beliefs. You will learn to use this skill to help you tolerate the tension you feel as you move towards your goal and when you experience a setback, to stop you from sabotaging your goal and giving in. Disputing in itself does not create a shift in your emotions, but it does motivate you to work to change them.

What do you dispute?

You dispute the four unhealthy or irrational beliefs that are triggered when you experience discomfort or a setback and you find yourself stuck as a result. As noted previously, the unhealthy belief about discomfort or setback may not include the four irrational beliefs, so you dispute the unhealthy beliefs that apply to your situation. You will recall that the four unhealthy beliefs are:

- the demand that you 'must' or 'have to'
- awfulizing
- low frustration tolerance
- self-/other-damning

After you dispute your unhealthy belief about discomfort or a setback, your next task is to dispute the healthy counterpart beliefs, namely:

- preference (I want to but I don't have to)
- anti-awfulizing (bad but not the end of the world)
- high frustration tolerance (difficult but I can stand it)
- self-/other-acceptance (I am worthwhile but fallible/You are worthwhile but fallible).

What is disputation based on?

Disputation is usually based on three major arguments:

1. Evidence that your unhealthy belief is inconsistent with reality. According to CBT there is no evidence to support any of the four unhealthy beliefs.

2. Logic. You refer to your healthy belief and ask if your unhealthy belief follows logically from it.
3. Helpfulness. You ask yourself to think about the effects of maintaining and believing your unhealthy belief and compare them with the effects of holding and strengthening your healthy belief.

At this point you may find it helpful to go back to Chapter 2 to remind yourself of the reasons why unhealthy beliefs are untrue, illogical and unhelpful and why healthy beliefs are true, logical and helpful to you. What you will learn now is how to apply these three arguments to both your unhealthy and healthy beliefs about discomfort and setbacks.

Go through the following exercise and then answer the disputing questions. Learn the disputing questions by heart because you can then use them whenever you want to challenge any unhealthy beliefs.

Exercise

1. Work out your goal about the feeling of discomfort or about any potential setback. For example, 'I want to be resilient and strong when I'm experiencing discomfort or setbacks. I want to achieve this change in three months. I want to tolerate discomfort and keep my focus on my goal.'
2. Identify the emotion you feel about being uncomfortable or about a potential setback. For example, 'I feel anxiety about the feeling of discomfort or possible setback when I'm applying my goal strategies.'

---

3. Identify the unhealthy belief you have about the feeling of discomfort or about the potential setback. For example, 'I have to feel comfortable when I'm applying my goal strategies. I can't stand feeling uncomfortable', or 'I must not experience any setbacks because that would prove that I'm useless'.

4. Identify the healthy belief you would like to have about the feeling of discomfort or about the potential setback. For example, 'I'd like to feel comfortable when I'm applying my change strategies. Feeling uncomfortable is challenging but I can stand it', or 'I'd like not to experience any setbacks but I accept that I might. If I do it never means I'm useless. I'm fallible but remain worthy regardless.'

Disputing the DEMAND . . .

Using evidence	• Is there a law that states you MUST feel comfort or MUST not experience a setback?
Using logic	• Just because you would like to be comfortable or would rather not experience a setback, does it make sense to insist that therefore you MUST feel comfort or that you MUST not experience a setback?
Using helpfulness	• How does believing that you MUST feel comfort or that you MUST not experience a setback help you to achieve what you want in the long term?

Disputing the AWFULIZING belief . . .

Using evidence	• Is it really true that it is AWFUL if you do not feel comfortable or experience a setback so bad that nothing worse could happen?
Using logic	• Just because you find discomfort or a setback bad, does it make sense to conclude that discomfort or a setback is the worst thing that can happen to you?

| Using helpfulness | • How is believing that discomfort or a setback is AWFUL going to help you to achieve what you want in the long term? |

Disputing the LOW FRUSTRATION TOLERANCE (LFT) belief . . .

Using evidence	• Is it really true that you CANNOT STAND/CANNOT COPE WITH/CANNOT BEAR discomfort or a setback? • Is there a law that states that discomfort or a setback is UNBEARABLE or something that you CANNOT STAND/TOLERATE?
Using logic	• Does it make sense to conclude that discomfort or a setback is something you cannot stand or tolerate?
Using helpfulness	• How is believing that discomfort or a setback is unbearable or something you cannot cope with going to help you achieve what you want in the long term? • Is believing that discomfort or a setback is unbearable/not something you can cope with going to help or hinder you in your pursuit of your long-term goal?

Disputing the SELF-DAMNING belief . . .

Using evidence	• Is it really true that you are useless/weak/worthless just because you feel discomfort or experience a setback? • Is there a law that states you become a useless/weak/worthless person just for feeling uncomfortable or for experiencing a setback?
Using logic	• Does it make sense to conclude that you are now useless/weak/worthless?
Using helpfulness	• How does believing that you are useless/weak/worthless just because you feel uncomfortable or because you experience a setback help you to achieve what you want in the long term? • Is believing that you are useless/weak/worthless just because you feel uncomfortable or because you experience a setback going to help or hinder you in your pursuit of your long-term goal?

Disputing the PREFERENCE belief . . .

Using evidence	• Is it true that you would like to feel comfort or not experience a setback, but you accept that it is possible that you might? Why it is true?
Using logic	• Even though you would like to be comfortable or would rather not experience a setback, does it make sense to conclude that it is not possible to always be comfortable and never experience setbacks? Why does it make sense?
Using helpfulness	• How is believing that you would like to feel comfort, or that you would like not to experience a setback, while accepting that it is possible that you might experience discomfort, or experience a setback, going to help you achieve what you want in the long term?
	• Is believing that you would like to experience comfort, or that you would like not to experience a setback, but accepting that it is possible that you might experience discomfort, or experience a setback, going to help or hinder you in your pursuit of your long-term goal?
	• How would it help?

Disputing the ANTI-AWFULIZING belief . . .

Using evidence	• Is it true that it is bad but not AWFUL if you do not feel comfortable or if you experience a setback? Why is it true?
Using logic	• Even though you find discomfort or experiencing a setback bad, does it make sense to conclude that discomfort or a setback is not the worst thing that can happen?
	• Why does it make sense?
Using helpfulness	• How is believing that feeling discomfort, or experiencing a setback, is bad but not awful, going to help you achieve what you want in the long term?
	• Is believing that feeling discomfort or experiencing a setback is bad but not awful going to help or hinder you in your pursuit of your long-term goal?
	• How would it help?

Disputing the *HIGH FRUSTRATION TOLERANCE (HFT)* belief . . .

Using evidence	• Is it true that you find it difficult but that you CAN STAND/COPE WITH/BEAR discomfort or a setback? Why is it true?
Using logic	• Even though you find feeling discomfort or experiencing a setback difficult or bad, does it make sense to conclude that feeling discomfort or experiencing a setback is something you can stand or tolerate? Why does it make sense?
Using helpfulness	• How is believing that feeling discomfort or experiencing a setback is hard, but not unbearable or something you cannot cope with, going to help you to achieve what you want in the long term?
	• Is believing that feeling discomfort or experiencing a setback is hard but not unbearable, and is something you can cope with, going to help or hinder you in your pursuit of your long-term goal?
	• Why would it help?

Disputing the *SELF-ACCEPTANCE* belief . . .

Using evidence	• Is it really true that you are not useless/weak/worthless just because you feel discomfort or because of a setback? Why is it true?
Using logic	• Just because you do not feel comfortable or because you experience a setback, does it make sense to conclude that you are not a useless/weak/worthless person?
	• Why does it make sense?
Using helpfulness	• How is believing that you are not a useless/weak/worthless person just because you feel uncomfortable or because you experience a setback going to help you achieve what you want in the long term?
	• Is believing that you are not a useless/weak/worthless person just because you feel uncomfortable or because you experience a setback going to help or hinder you in your pursuit of your long-term goal?
	• Why does it help?

Tips

As a general rule, use the arguments that you understand most easily. You can use just one or all of them. I have found that the helpfulness argument is not only easier to grasp but also seems to work more effectively than the others.

Metaphoric disputing

Metaphoric disputing involves using imagery to prove to yourself that your unhealthy belief about discomfort and setbacks is unhelpful and that your healthy belief about discomfort and setbacks is healthy. Unlike other disputing techniques, metaphoric disputing also enables you to shift your emotions more easily because it is vivid and emotive.

Metaphoric disputing involves using your imagination to create an image of both your unhealthy and your healthy belief about discomfort or setback. The image can be whatever best represents your beliefs. The second step is to imagine yourself in your unhealthy belief, looking at the world through its eyes, then stepping out of it, entering your healthy belief and looking at the world through the eyes of your healthy belief.

In both parts you should feel the emotions triggered by each belief so you can really understand what negative feelings it causes: an uncomfortable state with the unhealthy belief and an empowered state with the healthy belief. Then you imagine burning your unhealthy belief out of your mind as finally you commit to and accept your healthy belief.

The following steps outline the technique for using metaphoric disputing.

1. Write down your goal and healthy belief about resiliency.
2. Sit or lie down.

3. Close your eyes.
4. Breathe in deeply, hold it for three or four seconds and then breathe out gently. Repeat this five or six times.
5. Create an image that represents your unhealthy belief and an image that represents your healthy belief about discomfort or a setback.
6. Imagine these two images side by side in your mind.
7. Imagine stepping inside the unhealthy belief image as you recite it in your mind.
8. Become aware of how you think and feel and how you see yourself with the eyes of your unhealthy belief.
9. As you recite your healthy belief about discomfort or a setback imagine stepping out of the unhealthy belief image and stepping inside your healthy belief image.
10. Become aware of how you think and feel as you see yourself with the eyes of your healthy belief.
11. Imagine stepping out of your healthy belief image.
12. Imagine burning the unhealthy belief image until no trace of it is left.
13. Imagine drawing the healthy belief image and then recite 'this is the new me now'.
14. Open your eyes.

Repeat this technique daily to strengthen your resiliency.

You have now learned how to prepare and plan for seeing yourself as resilient and strong. If you have followed all the exercises, you have done enough mental preparation, and in the next chapter you will learn about taking action.

8
Taking Action and Responsibility

So far, most of the work has been cognitive, but there comes a point when you need to take action. For example, it is impossible to get fit by sitting at home imagining yourself in the gym. You need to start going to the gym, not just once or twice but regularly. Maintaining a momentum of action is vital. Or, if you want to have a lovely garden, you need to go out and start doing the dirty work, not just once and only when the weather is good, but regularly. After your garden blooms, you need to maintain it or the weeds will grow back. For maximum effectiveness, what you need to do is to take action and maintain the momentum after you have reflected, challenged and changed your beliefs and thoughts.

In this chapter you will learn about creating actions that enable you to achieve your goals. You will learn about reviewing your progress and learning from mistakes and failures so that you can develop and grow as a person while remaining focused on your goal. In this way, you will continue to add to your tool kit as you move on, and experience how mistakes and failures really do become opportunities to do better next time. It's natural to feel upset at first, but as long as your beliefs remain healthy and rational you can add what you have learned to your resources and try again with more knowledge and skills.

ACCOUNTABILITY AND ACTION

You might associate accountability with problems and blame, usually with negative connotations. Accountability really means taking responsibility without blame. Responsibility means understanding what is down to you, making a judgement about what you did or didn't do but without judging your worth. Blame, on the other hand, involves making a judgement about your worth as a human being, which is unhelpful in terms of personal development and growth or goal achievement. You already know that self-damning provokes depression, anxiety, unhealthy anger, guilt and hurt, none of which help you to think in a healthy and constructive way.

Accountability means taking responsibility for your goals, and realizing that you are choosing to have these goals and owning them. You also own the actions you are prepared to take in making them happen. Essentially, 'if it's to be, then it's up to me'. When you take responsibility and make yourself accountable for your goals and actions, you can assess how well you are doing and learn from the experience. If you give the responsibility to someone else, you become dependent instead of being free. Accountability gives you the freedom to do what you are choosing to do.

You may say that not everything is in your control, and you would be right; however, what you do and feel about it when something is outside your control – whether you tolerate the situation or take action – is up to you. For example, if a friend lets you down a lot, then your friend is responsible for their behaviour, but you are responsible for continuing to feel let down. Making yourself accountable will allow you to truly understand the role you play in what happens in your life and what you can achieve.

Taking action is an important part of accountability. You have worked on your goals and now it's time to do something about them. If you do not take action then you are not taking responsibility for making your goals happen.

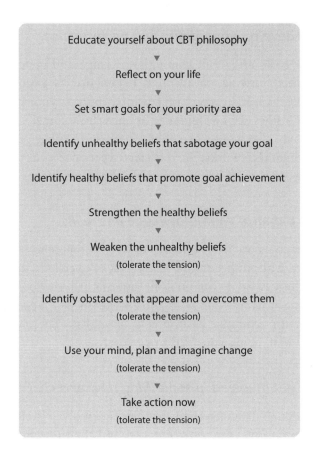

Educate yourself about CBT philosophy
▼
Reflect on your life
▼
Set smart goals for your priority area
▼
Identify unhealthy beliefs that sabotage your goal
▼
Identify healthy beliefs that promote goal achievement
▼
Strengthen the healthy beliefs
▼
Weaken the unhealthy beliefs
(tolerate the tension)
▼
Identify obstacles that appear and overcome them
(tolerate the tension)
▼
Use your mind, plan and imagine change
(tolerate the tension)
▼
Take action now
(tolerate the tension)

You have worked on setting goals and on changing your beliefs. Because you set a SMART goal you also have a target date for achieving it. Now it is time to take action. This involves planning and knowing the activities you will need to do in order to make your goal happen. The preceding flowchart summarizes the process so far with the addition of taking action.

When you think about your goals you might realize that they can be broken down into the three areas listed below. Whatever area they come into, the above process still applies:

1. To develop your ability and performance

These goals are about gaining knowledge and understanding and then moving on through experience to become more competent. Initially you would want to increase your knowledge about, raise your awareness of or know how something works. You may also want to be able to explain to other people how the something works. As you gain experience your goals may change to include being more able and more effective.

2. To enhance your knowledge and skills

These goals involve building on your competence and skills. They are about becoming very good, or excellent, or even the best there is. So if your goals fit into this criteria you would be looking at using your skills and competence in more complex ways, for example becoming a specialist. These goals are about enhancing your skills or expertise.

3. To get involved in something new and challenging

These goals are concerned with getting involved in challenging new situations, tasks or ventures, and then developing your skills so you can succeed in them. These types of goals may involve retraining or gaining new experiences.

The actions you now take should fit in with your goals and the areas your goals fall into. There are many types of different actions you can take. The following guidelines are just some examples that can apply to work or to non-work-related goals.

Doing new and different things

Look for new opportunities in what you are already doing, so that you can learn and develop. For example, if you are looking to develop within your present job, you could do new things and expand your existing role by talking to your manager.

Short-term role changes

Rotate with another person to enhance your skills, stand in for a colleague, or get seconded to another team within your area of work.

Shadowing

Watch and learn from a colleague or more experienced person. Shadowing is part of the training process in many industries, such as teaching or the airline business.

Coaching or supervision

Get one-to-one support from an expert to learn and improve existing skills. In the business world this is commonly referred to as coaching. In psychological services it is often referred to as supervision or clinical supervision but the objective is the same.

Distance learning

If at the moment your time is limited by your 9-to-5 working day, learn something new at your own pace. There are many courses that can help you to enhance your current knowledge or learn something completely new, for example IT skills. You can also find information on your specific interest in books, journals and on the internet.

Personal development

As you strive towards your goals, you may become aware of deeper rooted psychological challenges that require more than self-help books, which may mean finding an experienced therapist. Remember it is important that you choose the right type of therapy so the best thing would be to seek a medical or psychiatric referral or word-of-mouth recommendation.

Networking

If you are keen on developing your professional life or work goals, you could seek to build both internal and external contacts. Outside your work environment you can probably find many groups that meet regularly and exchange business information within an informal setting.

Challenging tasks

The most effective way to expand your comfort zone is to commit yourself to doing something challenging. If, for example, you have been working on performance anxiety problems, such as talking in front of an audience, then after you have done your cognitive preparation, volunteer to do the next presentation at work or make a sales pitch, or introduce yourself to new colleagues. Or you might commit yourself to a deadline or a new project and start it today.

Immediate tasks

Think about what you can do right now in order to kick-start action. For example, writing a letter, making a phone call or filling in the application form that has been waiting on your desk for the last month.

Additional training or workshops

If you want to find information about something that is of interest to you, you can find out if there are taster courses or, if you want to further enhance your skills, you can start attending workshops. In almost everything that you want to do, you will find that you can always develop your skills further.

Further qualifications

If you are interested in changing direction or simply wishing to further your professional or academic qualifications, there are many routes open to you.

Other interests

This is a catch-all area for your external interests, for example charity work, clubs or groups for professional reasons, sport and leisure.

Free advice

Government and private agencies offer free advice in many areas. For example, many banks provide leaflets on writing a business plan and offer advice and guidance on starting a new business.

Exercise

Now that you have worked on your beliefs and feel that you are ready to expand your comfort zone by taking action, think of the actions that you can take today.

Write your SMART goal.

Write the overall target date for achieving your goal. Write down your healthy beliefs.

Make a list of the immediate actions you can take. Do not wait for tomorrow or next week.

Write down all your action ideas to enable you to achieve your goal.

For example:

- *Talk to my family about what I want to do.*
- *Get relevant information about the course I'm interested in.*
- *Ring the bank to make an appointment to discuss a loan.*

BE OPEN AND LEARN FROM FAILURES AND DISAPPOINTMENT

When you start taking action towards achieving your goal, and after you have started strengthening your healthy beliefs and weakening your unhealthy beliefs, you will feel a mixture of tension and excitement.

You will feel tension because you may be stretching your comfort zone – which is good – and excitement because you are doing something positive by taking action.

Most of the things you have done so far have involved learning and being open-minded. When you started reading this book, you learned about some aspects of CBT. As you continued you learned more specific ideas and how to use your cognitive skills. Some of the concepts may have been thought-provoking or challenging at first, but you kept an open mind and continued learning. You will now need these two specific resources as you start taking action – being open-minded and learning from your experiences.

Being open-minded is an excellent trait to develop because it allows you to remain receptive to new opportunities and possibilities – and that means more resources to achieve your goal. However, if you stick to one way of doing things even when you have the chance to learn about other options, then you limit your ability to achieve your goal. So stay open-minded because usually there are much better and more effective options.

Remember the diagram below? If you believe that you have nothing further to learn then you become closed and unconsciously incompetent, and you stop looking for new ideas and ways to learn and improve.

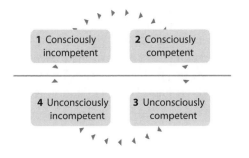

When you start to take action, bear in mind the fact that you are stretching your comfort zone. Looking at the above diagram, remember you may be starting from point 1, so the likelihood of disappointment and failure is quite high. You will become more experienced and more successful if you stay open-minded and learn from your experiences.

The diagram below illustrates the learning process.

Example

Tom wants to make a smooth and confident presentation to his colleagues at work. He has been working on changing his anxiety-provoking beliefs regarding presentation and has now volunteered to do the next team presentation as part of his action-taking plan. His presentation is on improving customer services.

After his presentation Tom applies the learning process by asking the following questions:

What did I want to achieve?

I wanted to achieve a smooth and confident presentation.

What did I achieve?

I achieved a presentation which was good. It was not as smooth and confident as I would have liked. I didn't get the kind of response I wanted regarding my suggestions on improving customer services. My manager said 'well done'.

Reflect on the experience

The experience was good because I knew I was out of my comfort zone. I am just starting to do presentations so it is understandable that I have lots to learn. I am happy that my manager said 'well done'. I felt uncomfortable at the beginning but then I relaxed. After the presentation was over, I did worry about it a little.

I did not invite a discussion on my suggestions for improving customer services and I did not ask for feedback about my presentation.

What can I learn?

I know that I can now stand in front of people and present. It will take time to be confident because I'm just starting. My discomfort was natural and understandable because I am continuing to strengthen my healthy beliefs and weaken my unhealthy beliefs.

I can be more interactive when I'm presenting and invite people to contribute. This would make it more interesting.

What would I do differently next time?

I will volunteer again and next time I will ask questions and invite people to discuss any ideas I present.

I will also ask my manager to give me feedback on what I can improve in the presentation.

I will ensure that I counteract any feelings of worry by reciting my healthy belief and ensuring that my thoughts and self-talk remain constructive.

I will continue to use the imagery techniques to deal with negative outcomes and see myself at my best.

Exercise

Reflect on what you wanted to achieve from the actions that you have taken.

What did you achieve in reality? Be honest and realistic.

Reflect on the experiences you had when you took action and think of both the positive and the negative of the experiences.

What did you learn from your reflection? Be constructive. What would you do differently next time?

ACKNOWLEDGE AND EXPRESS YOUR FEELINGS APPROPRIATELY

When you start to take action you will either achieve what you wanted to achieve completely, partly or not at all. Whatever you achieve you will experience a feeling about it, and this is natural. You may experience happiness and excitement, mixed feelings or disappointment and upset. Whatever you feel, it is important to learn to express it appropriately. Striving for your goals does not mean you become an unfeeling robot, always positive and upbeat. What you are aiming for is to acknowledge and express your emotions in a healthy and appropriate way.

You read about the ABC model of emotional disturbance and how sometimes AC expressions are used. This is when you make the cause of your emotions the very experience that you have just had, or are having, or might have. AC language essentially says: 'I'm not responsible for my emotions but he or she or it is.'

A	B	C
Event	Belief	Consequences
	Healthy or unhealthy	Emotions Behaviours Thoughts Symptoms

AC language is when you say or think:

- *He made me angry.*
- *My job makes me depressed.*
- *You upset me.*

It is clear that there is no emotional responsibility in AC language. When you start to take action it is important that you learn to express your feelings appropriately for a number of reasons. Firstly, you will be feeling something, and keeping it bottled up is unhealthy. Secondly, the appropriate expression of your emotional response plays a part in strengthening or weakening your belief in your emotional responsibility and accountability. For example, if your application for a loan or a job is turned down and you tell yourself, 'filling an application form and sending it in makes me nervous because I was turned down the last time', what exactly are you implying? When you reflect about that expression it's easy to see there is a deeper implication. Repeating that type of expression would condition you to think unhealthily again.

How to express your emotions

Emotions can be expressed appropriately when you own them. This means thinking and talking in a responsible and empowered way. For example:

- *I feel anxious about . . .*
- *I felt angry when . . .*
- *I am upset about . . .*
- *I am happy about . . .*
- *I am excited about . . .*

Avoid expressions like:

- *You make me anxious . . .*
- *You made me angry when . . .*
- *This makes me depressed . . .*

It is extremely important to have good communication and to express your emotions appropriately, particularly when you are working in partnership with other people.

Certain expressions can be a trigger for a defensive response from others. Can you remember a time when, for example, someone gave you feedback about something that you did or didn't do or about your performance, and you were told 'you made me feel anxious', or 'you make me angry'?

It's not surprising that you may have felt defensive and perhaps equally attacking. In constructive communication, appropriate expressions would be:

- *I felt anxious when you said . . .*
- *I felt angry when you behaved . . .*
- *I felt sad that you were . . .*

When the emotional response belongs firmly to you, the other person is unlikely to feel attacked or defensive and they can then respond more calmly or healthily.

When you have achieved what you wanted

When you have achieved your goal, acknowledge it positively and also recognize the help that you have been given along the way from other people. It is important that you acknowledge your achievement and pat yourself on the back for your success. This is as important as learning from your mistakes. It is good to tell yourself that you have done well and that you are proud of yourself. It is also good to acknowledge those who have supported you or have contributed to your success. Celebrate your achievements because it will feel good and reinforce and strengthen your conviction in your own ability.

If someone compliments you on your success or achievements, accept it positively. In the past you may have tended to dismiss compliments but now you can send a clear and positive signal to yourself about your own abilities by acknowledging compliments from others. Initially, you may feel awkward, but you are simply being polite and respectful to the person who is being generous enough to compliment you. Once you have accepted the compliment then internalize it.

When you have partly achieved what you wanted

When you have partly achieved what you wanted, acknowledge what you are feeling about it. You may feel a healthy negative emotion like disappointment, annoyance, regret, concern or sadness. You may also feel unhealthy negative emotions like hurt, unhealthy anger, embarrassment, anxiety or depression.

If your feelings are healthily negative, you may need a few days before you are ready to reflect objectively. Healthy negative emotions will heal and you will soon re-focus on your goal. You will know that you are experiencing healthy negative emotions because your thoughts and behaviours will still be constructive and healthy.

Once you have acknowledged your feelings, consider the things that went well and the things that didn't.

Acknowledge the things that you did well and reinforce them by being positive about them. It is important that you have a sense of balance about what has happened. Most of the time you will find that some things went well, so affirm that was the case. Learn from what did not go well and then think about what you will do differently next time. This will provide a progressive action plan that is fluid and forward moving.

If your feelings are unhealthily negative, it means you have an unhealthy belief about what has happened. You will know that your feelings are unhealthily negative because you will feel stuck and unable to move forward or to let go. Your thoughts and behaviours will not be healthy or constructive.

If your feelings are unhealthily negative, you will need to identify the unhealthy belief(s) and start by challenging it and working on its healthy version. You will then need to strengthen the healthy version and weaken the unhealthy version. Essentially you will apply the CBT process you have been learning.

Once you make the change to your beliefs then you will be able to think more objectively, as if you have healthy negative emotions.

When you have not achieved what you wanted

When you have not achieved what you wanted you may experience either a healthy negative emotion or an unhealthy negative emotion.

Once you have acknowledged your healthy negative feelings, sit down and reflect on what happened. Think about what you have learned and what you will do differently the next time.

If your feelings are unhealthily negative, you need to change the unhealthy beliefs causing them. Reflect on what happened in a constructive manner, identify what you learned and what you will do differently the next time.

DECISION MAKING

In order for you to achieve your goals you will need to take appropriate risks. This involves decision making. The decision is either to do or not to do something. It is about staying put and not making any change, or making the decision to pursue your goals and desires. In order for you to make this decision you have to weigh up the costs and benefits of making a change or whether or not to strive for your goal.

Life is full of risk and you cannot totally eliminate it from your life. There is an element of risk in everything you do, whether it is crossing the street, getting into a car, doing a presentation, eating something or getting ill. Even if you decide to stay in bed and not do anything, life is still risky. The bottom line is that in order for you to achieve something, you will need to take risks by taking action and making a decision. Being totally risk free is unfeasible.

However, the degree of risk you are willing to take will depend on you. You may be a high risk-taker or a very cautious person. Your attitude to risk and how much risk you take will impact on the decisions you make and ultimately on what you may achieve.

Having healthy beliefs means that you are psychologically strong enough to pursue your goal and deal with the possibility of not achieving it in a constructive way so that you can re-focus on it later. So the starting point is with your attitude and belief system.

Working on strengthening your healthy beliefs will enable you to be more objective about making decisions and pursuing your goals.

1. First you set a **SMART** goal.
2. Begin to gather information about what is actually involved in the process, educating yourself, learning

about concepts of psychological health and the process of change. At this stage you will really decide if it is something that you wish to invest in or not.

3. If you decide that it is significant enough to pursue, you then begin to plan. To change your unhealthy beliefs, you start to plan by using your cognitive skills.

4. After you plan, you then take action. This is the doing part of the behavioural change that you are undertaking.

5. Then you assess how you did and learn from it.

Point 2 above explains appropriate risk, reflecting on your decision and then committing to your goal or an option. You can assess this dilemma more effectively if you apply a simple business technique called cost benefit analysis. As the name implies, you will be assessing the cost and benefit of either taking a risk and pursuing your desire or not, or simply deciding between two options and assessing which you feel is more desirable to you at a given point in your life.

Once you have considered the costs and the benefits you can then reflect more objectively on how you wish to proceed or which option to commit to.

The following is a simple form you can use when you wish to weigh up the pros and cons.

You can see that this form takes into account the advantages and disadvantages of not making a change, and the advantages and disadvantages of making a change or choosing the goal

Option/Problem 1		Option/Problem 2	
Advantages/Benefits		Advantages/Benefits	
Short term	Long term	Short term	Long term

Option/Problem 1		Option/Problem 2	
Disadvantages/Costs		Disadvantages/Costs	
Short term	Long term	Short term	Long term

in both the short and in the long term. This is extremely important because often you will find that you may make a decision based on how you are feeling now. If you remember that striving and pursuing your goals will feel uncomfortable at first, it helps to focus your mind on the long term so that your decision is based on the end result and not just short-term discomfort.

DO IT AGAIN

You will have realized that throughout this book concepts are repeated in different ways. Repetition is vital, just like learning from your experiences and then doing it again.

The process of goal attainment involves focusing on your goal and overcoming hurdles along the way. These hurdles come in numerous guises but the main point is that you can overcome many of them and accept those that you cannot without letting go of your goal, as long as it stays significant for you. So, at first, if you fail, reflect on the experience, assess it objectively, learn from it and do it again with what you have learned firmly at the forefront of your mind.

To assess the reality of continuing to strive for your goal, consider the costs and benefits of it all. If the benefits outweigh the costs to you, you can do it again and again. This process of assessment should include the benefits and costs to the people in your life too, and provided you have thought about this, you can go ahead and make your choice.

When you learn from your experiences and decide to do it again, ensure that your feelings, thoughts and actions are in accordance with your healthy beliefs and attitudes. This is not being selfish or uncaring, simply accepting the consequences of your decisions in the right spirit of choice and accountability.

9
Accepting the Possibility of Failure and Disappointment

Failure and disappointment are universal human experiences. In order to achieve goals we need to dislike failure and disappointment but not be fearful of them. This chapter will help you learn how to accept failure and disappointment while remaining focused on your goals.

It is not uncommon for new businesses and ventures to fail in the first two years. The figures are surprising. Only between 15–20% last beyond the second year. Yet despite the fact that failure and disappointment happen, even more surprisingly they are not often discussed, as if mentioning failure and disappointment is unacceptable. Some schools banish competitive sports and discourage healthy competition because it is perceived that a) competitiveness is bad and b) children will fail – meaning that they will fail and then perceive themselves as failures. Children are then deprived of the opportunity to understand that they can deal with failing in a constructive way and learn something valuable that will serve them later on in adulthood. Instead, they receive the opposite message.

There is, however, a positive side to failure and disappointment. In many ways, they hold the key to your success.

In some Eastern philosophies good and bad are given equal weight. Life and death are seen as natural aspects of life. Success and failure and other opposites are not labelled as good and bad. Change, destruction and death are seen as part of the natural cycle; the problem does not lie with the forces themselves but with your reactions to them. Failure, or the challenge of failure and disappointment, can be seen as either a reason for despair or as an aid to personal development and emotional growth, learning or even spiritual development.

Any risk you undertake in life brings with it the possibility of failure or disappointment. This happens whenever you wish to make any change.

Accepting failure is about accepting your fallibility as a human being. No one is perfect. Perfection is something that does not exist. What does exist is excellence and striving for excellence. Perfection means that nothing better exists, or that you have reached a stage of knowledge where you have learned everything and no one can surpass you. If you believe that you have reached your own level of perfection, this is the opposite of catastrophizing (when you believe that nothing worse can exist). Neither of these concepts is consistent with reality. The truth is you can improve and worse things can happen.

In the traditions of the Navaho tribe, rugs and blankets are woven with a knot in them as a reminder that humankind is not perfect. By weaving a knot, they believe they are ensuring that the gods are not angered by humans thinking that they are like gods. Human fallibility, making mistakes or failing is represented by the knot, a visible reminder that shows how imperfection might be reflected upon and accepted.

FAILURE AND FAILING

There are three aspects to consider when thinking about failure. Firstly, there is failure. Secondly, there is failing. Thirdly, there is your role in the failure or the failing. The diagram below illustrates this. There are four possibilities:

1. Failure has occurred and you are fully or partly responsible.
2. Failure has occurred but it was not your responsibility at all.
3. Something is failing and you are fully or partly responsible.
4. Something is failing but it is not your responsibility.

	My responsibility	Not my responsibility
Failure	Yes/No	Yes/No
Failing	Yes/No	Yes/No

Failure is tangible. You know that you have failed at something or in something. For example, you may have failed at losing weight, or in your business, exam or relationship. It is much easier to know that you have failed than to recognize that you are failing in something or at something. Even when you recognize you are failing, you may decide to keep going because you do not want to give up, for example, in your relationship or in your work performance.

How far you are prepared to persist eventually leads you to decide when to throw in the towel and accept that something is not working. There is no shame in changing your mind. It is excellent to persist but it is also important to be smart. When faced with such decisions it is always good to consider doing a cost benefit analysis as shown in Chapter 8.

Being goal-directed does not mean that the option of choosing to quit something should be out of the question. It is all a matter of balance.

Successful business people not only know how to be creative and goal-directed but they also check if their efforts are rewarded and they are smart enough to know when to stop and start something else.

How far you persist is down to you. You can of course keep at it, but recognize the costs in terms of time, money, new ventures, family and other personal circumstances. If you have been working at something for years, investing time, money and creativity, and you are still failing, reflect on it first and then conduct a thorough cost benefit analysis. It may even be worth investing in external help when making the assessment. If what you are failing at involves other people, then everyone who is involved is required to be part of the decision-making process. For example, if your relationship is failing then both you and your partner need to consider why, and to ask what you want. You can only do so much and your partner's goals are outside of your responsibility. Provided that both of you want to work on your relationship and to make improvements, there are possibilities – but if one of you has already opted out, your responsibility becomes whether you wish to persist or not.

The previous diagram will help you to consider whether failure or failing is within your responsibility or if it is someone else's responsibility. The important thing is to be honest with yourself first.

Accepting responsibility for failure and failing

Failure and failing at something is not a pleasant experience but no one is exempt from it. Failure and failing is not an indication of your worth as a person. Accepting responsibility for your failure and failing does not mean that you become a failure as a person.

Taking responsibility is an indication of emotional maturity and growth. This doesn't mean damning yourself as a failure or labelling yourself as worthless. That is totally unhealthy, illogical and unhelpful.

The first thing is to acknowledge the failure and failing without making excuses or shifting the responsibility onto someone else. Accepting responsibility provides you with the opportunity to see what you can do and as a consequence take more control of your life. It gives you an opportunity to learn and move on so that you can make better choices in the future.

Accepting responsibility for failure and failing may trigger intense but natural emotions. You may experience mixed emotions. You can identify your feelings and then set to work on the belief you hold that is causing them. It is not the failure or the failing but your response to it that matters. You can change your emotional response as it is provoked by your beliefs, and they are within your control.

You can learn and become more experienced but you will never eliminate failure or failing from your life. However, you can learn not to be disturbed when this happens.

Accepting failure and failing when they are out of your control

Sometimes, and despite your excellent efforts and healthy attitude, failure and failing still occur. This happens because there are factors outside your control.

In such circumstances, accepting the things that are out of your control is as important as taking responsibility for what you can control. Once again, your response to failures and failing is within your control. You can either respond healthily or unhealthily.

Remember there is usually something to learn even in the projects that have failed due to factors that were outside your control. Perhaps you learned how to write a better report or a business plan, network more successfully, or apply for funding. This becomes more obvious once you have untangled your emotional knots about the failure or failing.

Not accepting failure and failing

There are always people who say that not accepting failure was the solution to their success, or that failure was not an option for them and that is why they managed to overcome an illness or some other obstacle. Using a combination of resiliency and effort they continued to strive for their goal.

Often they simply rejected the suggestion that they were a failure.

For example, a child living in an extremely difficult environment may be told that he won't amount to much or that he is stupid. Incredibly, some of these children grow up to be great sportsmen and women and become high achievers. The reality is often that they did not accept the negative suggestions. Some say, 'it made me more determined to prove them wrong'. What they all have in common is that they worked very hard to learn and improve their situation.

Learning and improving is all about recognizing that perfection does not exist and that you are fallible. It is about not seeing failure or fallibility as a catastrophe. It means possibly making wrong choices and mistakes and then realizing that there are other things you can do despite initial limitations or hardships.

There is a difference between having a fighting spirit and not accepting failure. A fighting spirit helps you stay focused on your goal. Not accepting failure leads to anxiety and disturbance: two very different outcomes.

What happens when you fail?

Failure can trigger many different emotions in you.

You can have a healthy negative emotional response or an unhealthy negative emotional response. The unhealthy emotional response will be provoked by your unhealthy beliefs that will trigger you to feel as if you are stuck and unable to move forward. The healthy negative emotional response will feel painful and stressful, but you will then move forward and be able to reflect on the failure with an objective mind. If your emotional response was unhealthy you may experience the following:

1. Not accepting the reality of failure
This is usually experienced as numbness or shock and at first you may be in denial, saying, 'I can't believe it happened'. You may not yet feel any emotions. You haven't yet accepted the reality of what has happened. This can last a few days or even longer. If this stage persists for a long time and you are still in shock about what has happened, you may need professional help. Not feeling anything when you have failed at something that was very significant is unhealthy. Sooner or later you would need to deal with what is being blocked or avoided. In the long term the pain of facing the reality will be worth it.

If, however, you get over the initial shock, then you will feel negative emotions.

2. Feeling the negative emotions
Experiencing negative emotions is natural, so allow yourself to experience them. You will not know at this point whether they are the product of a healthy or an unhealthy belief. The best thing to do is to allow your feelings and talk to friends and family and people who can support you. It is natural to be vulnerable and out of sync at this stage.

3. Time Limited Irrationality
When you experience failure (and depending on how significant the consequence was to you) you may experience what is known as Time Limited Irrationality. This means that you can experience neurosis and irrationality for a short period

of time and it is quite normal, hence the time limited aspect of it. During this limited period you may talk, behave and think as if you have really unhealthy beliefs. You may find yourself catastrophizing, saying you can't bear it and how the experience means that you are useless. As long as it's for a short period of time, usually a few hours or a day, then this is a natural part of the acceptance and healing process.

If, however, the negative emotions do not change after weeks and if you find yourself thinking about the failure, feeling that you are stuck in a rut, or experiencing anger, anxiety, shame, depression, guilt or hurt, then you may now and with some confidence say that you have an unhealthy belief that requires your attention. If you feel stuck, start by applying the CBT process. Start with identifying what you are feeling and then identify the unhealthy beliefs provoking the emotion or emotions.

Common unhealthy emotions experienced when failure occurs

1. Anxiety
As explained earlier, anxiety is the unhealthy emotional response to threat and danger. You may be anticipating another failure or worry about other potential failures. Its healthy version is concern. Both anxiety and concern are essentially fear-based emotions. One is unhealthy and immobilizing and the other is balanced and realistic.

Here are some examples of what you may become anxious about following a failure:

- Finding another job if your employment was terminated for whatever reason.
- Paying your mortgage or bills.

- Finding another relationship if the current one has ended.
- Taking another exam if you failed a recent one.

Essentially you become anxious about failing again or about the consequences of the failure.

If you are feeling anxiety and not concern, you will probably be over-exaggerating the negative aspects of future failures and consequences. You may be thinking that you won't be able to cope if it happens again. When you are anxious you will tend to see the glass as half empty and your thinking will not be constructive or progressive. You will also feel like running away from the idea of starting again, and may notice that you are drinking more or numbing your emotions in other ways.

You can tackle your anxiety by facing what you are anxious about and then applying the CBT process to identify and change your anxiety-causing beliefs first.

2. Depression
Depression is the unhealthy psychological response to loss or to failure. Its healthy version is sadness.

When a goal is not achieved or when failure about other aspects of the goal occur, you may become depressed. You will recognize depression because you feel stuck in negativity about the failure. You will see the future as hopeless and believe that you are a failure too. Your thinking may be affected in that it becomes slower and you may feel lethargic and unmotivated. You will also be thinking about past failures which potentially reinforce your unhealthy beliefs.

Usually, anxiety and depression are experienced together. It is also possible that you become anxious about being depressed.

Sadness, on the other hand, is the healthy response to failure or to loss. The most obvious indicator of sadness is that you still feel hopeful about the future and you will not believe that you are a failure because you failed.

There are many different types of depression other than a specific reaction to failure. It is important that you seek professional and medical help in the first instance and then follow the CBT process of identifying and changing your depression-provoking beliefs.

3. Unhealthy anger

Anger is another common emotion experienced following a failure. You can experience unhealthy anger or healthy anger (annoyance) about your failure. Both are about rule-breaking. For example, you may think that you have broken a personal rule which then led to the failure or that someone else did. You might also feel angry towards life or the world because an unfairly perceived event occurred.

You can recognize unhealthy anger because you may be calling yourself, another, or the world, every name under the sun. This means that you may be making global negative judgements. You may also be thinking or behaving aggressively and unreasonably. You may perceive malice in other people's actions and believe that their bad actions were deliberate and personal. You may feel like avenging yourself.

Healthy anger is balanced. You tend to judge the action or the performance as opposed to judging yourself or someone else. You become assertive and objective about your disappointment. Healthy anger enables you to sit with your emotion rather than immediately expressing it by shouting or arguing. You give yourself time to think about the most constructive way of dealing with the problem.

4. Shame/embarrassment

Shame and embarrassment are also common emotional responses to failure when something becomes public knowledge, or if you see yourself or something that you have done in a certain way. The healthy version is regret.

If, for example, the failure and the circumstances around it became public, you might feel ashamed because of the risk of people thinking badly of you. You would link your worth to other people's negative judgement and begin to see yourself as unworthy.

If you tend to be anxious about negative judgement, you might feel ashamed or depressed or angry if negative judgement occurs after the failure. Anxiety is about what could happen in the future.

You would deal with your feeling of shame by using the CBT process to identify the shame-causing beliefs and then change them to regret-causing beliefs.

Other unhealthy emotions, like envy, hurt, jealousy and guilt, are also common in the event of failure. In the same way, the CBT process can be used to identify and change the unhealthy beliefs provoking these emotions. As always, the process of change is more significant than your specific emotional state when you are working on changing beliefs.

Why do you fail?

There is no universal answer to this question to fit every situation. Like everyone, you are fallible and not everything is within your control.

If you are fearful or anxious about failure you will tend to adopt unrealistic goals about yourself or your skills. Consequently, you will create a self-fulfilling prophecy where you expect to fail. This state of anxiety leads to avoidance and negative thinking and thus increases the chances of failing. High achievers, on the other hand, do not fear failure and they do not see it as an indication of low self-worth. If you are a high achiever you will dislike, but not feel anxious about, failure.

Anxiety about failure can start in childhood. You may have grown up in a family where high standards were expected. In such families, parents often demand that, for example, children succeed academically. Children then internalize demands such as, 'you must do better', 'you must try harder', 'you must succeed'. This leads to an unhealthy 'need' for success and not failing, which in turn causes unhealthy fear.

Be open and honest
In order to be able to identify these goal-sabotaging beliefs, you will need to be honest and open with yourself about the failure. If you blame it on someone else or ignore it, this will only reinforce your unhealthy beliefs. It may feel painful at first, but admitting to the failure is the first step to healing. If you do not declare the failure you will be blind to the solution, or to what you can learn from the situation.

Being open and honest about the failure with your family, close friends and those who matter to you provides you with the support and care you may need. It also helps as a reminder that the world has not ended and that you are still a valuable person. It helps you understand that you can, in fact, deal and cope with the failure.

Feel the pain and get up again

Allow yourself time to feel the pain and disappointment. Feeling pain and discomfort is natural and human. Do not kid yourself by pretending that you are immune to pain. It's OK and appropriate to have negative feelings. It is important that you do not catastrophize the failure. Tell yourself that it's hard and bad but that you will cope and deal with the difficulty and that the world has not ended. You will then keep a sense of proportion and see that hope and opportunities for learning still exist.

Once you have given yourself time to lick your wounds, you can then review what happened and develop a plan of action.

Learn from your failure and mistakes

You can now review your previous plans and identify where and when you deviated from them. You can take another look at the entire project and assess why the failure and mistakes happened. Remember that no one is perfect, so be prepared to accept responsibility but remain strong and learn from the failure and mistakes.

Work out what you have learned and how you would do things differently next time. What you learn should not be about paying someone back or about making unrealistic demands. Be constructive about what you have learned.

You failed – you are not a failure

One of the most significant things you can do is to see the failure as a failure, and yourself as fallible and worthwhile regardless. Remember that you failed but that you are not a failure as a person. Keep your worth detached from your performance. If you put yourself down and believe that you are now worthless and a failure you will end up depressing yourself about the failure and making yourself anxious about future failures.

Have a plan

Develop a plan of what to do and how to respond to the failure. This is not about giving up but about thinking and developing a plan of action. You may decide that you need additional skills so consider taking a course, for example, if that is what you need to do. If you work with others, you can agree a plan of action based on shared values and experiences.

Learn when to give up

There is no shame in knowing when to quit. It is far better to realize when a venture is not yielding results and knowing when to throw in the towel than continuing to invest time and effort in something that is clearly not working. In thinking about when to give up you can learn good business sense. Include this in your plans and contingencies.

Accepting disappointment

'We must accept finite disappointment, but never lose infinite hope.'

Martin Luther King, Jr

Dealing with disappointment is an important part of living. Life can be seen as a game of learning how to become stronger and more effective in the face of failure and disappointment. How you deal with both determines how much you succeed.

You experience disappointment when your goals are not achieved or when you fail. The goals you set for yourself, for others and the world around you can trigger feelings of disappointment when they are not realized.

Disappointment goes along with most of the negative emotions you feel. It can be expressed as depression, sadness, anger, annoyance, anxiety or concern.

You have learned that emotions can be healthily or unhealthily negative. When you experience a feeling of disappointment, the first thing to do is acknowledge it and then work out what it actually is that you are feeling, for example hurt or anxiety. Accept it, and know that as long as you have a goal, desire, preference, want, like, dislike, need or demand, you will experience the negative emotion of disappointment.

Accepting disappointment means acknowledging that you will experience the pain of negative emotions when your goals are not achieved. Feeling bad or disappointed is natural and should not be avoided by alcohol, drugs, food or other tranquilizers.

Not all negative feelings of disappointment are unhealthy. It is possible that you may view all negative feelings as bad and therefore attempt to block them or tranquilize them, but doing that only makes matters worse. The only way to heal your feelings of disappointment, healthy or unhealthy, is to accept the pain you are experiencing. Accept it and take ownership of it.

All painful feelings of disappointment are finite. This means they don't last forever, particularly if they are provoked by healthy beliefs. Unhealthy beliefs can trigger these painful feelings for much longer, but even then they won't last forever.

Adopting a healthy attitude to negative emotions means developing acceptance and hope, with an eye on the future.

No matter how many courses on positive thinking you take, no matter how much you visualize success, you will not rid yourself of disappointment completely. It is part of life.

Celebrate and enjoy success and accept feelings of disappointment.

Accept the challenges of life

It is true that sometimes you will experience more disappointments in life than others will. It is true that sometimes your choices will be limited. Accept the hand you are dealt as a first step. This does not mean telling yourself 'this is how my life will be', but 'this is how it is now but I will learn to move on from it'. This way you will remain open to future opportunities because your attitude is constructive and helpful.

Take action now

At some point you will need to take action and act in accordance with your healthy belief. Use your imagination to set yourself up for taking real action. You will experience tension and discomfort, but this is natural and you should not see it as inappropriate or something to be avoided. This way you will stretch your comfort zone and learn to be more effective and tolerant of change.

10

Developing a Healthy Philosophy of Balance

What is it that we are all looking for when we set goals and strive to achieve them? We are all seeking happiness. Happiness comes in many forms, including the feelings of confidence, satisfaction, calmness, relaxation and comfort. These are the emotions we want to feel. When we eat, exercise, work, get praised, challenge ourselves, or do something that benefits someone else, we are achieving a goal that triggers positive feelings. When we achieve what we want in life, the result is happiness.

The emphasis is on the 'want' and not the 'need'. Striving for your desires and preferences without needing them is the key to achieving your goals and feeling happy. When you turn your desires and wants into 'need', 'must', 'should', and 'have to', this is the point when you coerce. This is like doing something with your hands tied together, or feeling that you are being pushed into something and if you don't do it, something terrible will happen. Coerciveness caused by this attitude triggers anxiety and fear. Letting go of 'needing to' or 'having to' turns the energy into personal motivation.

Changing your beliefs, attitudes and philosophy of life in this way means you become free because it turns actions and goals into choices: your personal choice. As you begin to think and believe that you are living your life in accordance with your personal choice, you set yourself up for more success and happiness. In a nutshell, happiness becomes a choice.

Because happiness can be triggered by your own achievements and actions, it is within your control. It can also be triggered by events that are outside your control, for example winning the lottery or receiving an inheritance. However, if you wait for happiness that is triggered by events outside your control, you could be waiting a long time. Happiness that is triggered by your achievements and work is much more attainable. The key to this type of happiness is achievement supported by healthy beliefs that focus you on your wants and desires in a motivating and positive way, rather than by beliefs that push and coerce you into striving to achieve a goal through fear and anxiety.

We all like to be in a state of comfort as opposed to discomfort. This can be tricky because achieving goals requires you to do the work now in order to succeed later. Naturally this means that working and putting in effort is essential. This may feel uncomfortable at first.

If you focus only on achieving future goals, constantly working and putting in lots of effort, you will not feel very happy in the here and now. This will result in more stressful feelings. A philosophy of healthy balance is necessary so that you can experience happiness and enjoyment in the short term while you are working towards long-term goals.

SHORT-TERM COMFORT

It is easy to understand why you want to be in a state of comfort as opposed to discomfort. Comfort feels good. From an early age children are looked after, fed, clothed and soothed. Neglect, on the other hand, causes pain and harm. You grow up knowing that there are certain things you can do or have others do for you that encourage feelings of comfort.

If as a child you feel uncomfortable or fearful, your parents will look after you and remove the object of fear. You grow up learning that if you avoid something that provokes fear your feelings of fear will remain. If as a child the object of fear is not removed then you can traumatize yourself and grow up fearful. This is why children need to be nurtured and looked after.

This can also be a source of problems for adults. Emotional maturity will not be accomplished if the adult continues to engage in the same childhood strategies of either avoiding things that trigger feelings of discomfort, or having a need for others to make life comfortable. You may be giving in to comfort-seeking short-term strategies at the expense of your long-term gains and goals.

Functioning on short-term comfort leads to problems because maturity and future goal achievements require you to deal with discomfort, take responsibility, and put in effort to learn new things, get on with people you may not like, and do mundane tasks, as well as dealing with failure.

It can be very helpful to reflect on your attitudes to living and achieving by checking your thoughts and behaviour. If you are operating on short-term comfort you may rid yourself of feelings of discomfort by avoidance, use of alcohol or drugs, procrastination and a reliance on others to make life easy for you. You feel very uncomfortable when you are required to do things for yourself, to put in effort and hard work. You may get angry and sulk when people do not do things for you to make life easy. If your focus is short-term comfort, long-term goals will be very tough to achieve. Commitment and personal responsibility may be lacking in many areas because you may have a need for life to be easy. And since life is not easy and comfortable, you feel frustration towards life and other people who are not making your life easy.

The following are some examples of unhealthy beliefs that create short-term comfort-seeking strategies:

- *I have to be comfortable and not uncomfortable. Being uncomfortable is terrible, I can't stand it.*
- *Life must be easy for me. I can't stand the fact that life is hard. I am unlucky. Poor me.*
- *People must make life easy for me. It's terrible that they don't. I can't tolerate that.*
- *If I do anything about changing my life, it will be difficult, and will mean that I will always experience hardship – and I MUST not because that would be awful and unbearable.*

Exercise

Lucy is depressed about her weight problem and has tried every diet she has heard of. She gets very angry and frustrated when she reads about how celebrities lose a lot of weight easily. She thinks life is very unfair and feels pity for herself. Whenever she attempts to eat healthily, little and often, and attempts to exercise, her heart sinks and she gives up. She rationalizes her behaviour by saying that she doesn't enjoy exercising and finds it boring so that's why she stops. 'If only I enjoyed exercising then I would exercise and wouldn't have a problem', is a typical expression. She also says that she cannot control herself because chocolate is her weakness. 'My will-power just goes out of the window', is another favourite expression. As a consequence of her failure to lose the extra weight she has become depressed and sees herself as a total failure.

BREAKING THE PROBLEM DOWN

Lucy has mixed emotions of depression, anger and anxiety. The anxiety, experienced as discomfort and frustration, is avoided by giving up the healthy eating pattern and the exercise.

Her behaviour is avoidant in that she does not maintain her healthy eating. She gives it up and gives in to her immediate sense of gratification by having chocolate as and when she pleases. She also gives up on exercise because she finds it boring. Her intolerance of boredom and lack of enjoyment result in giving up easily.

Her thoughts justify her short-term comfort-seeking beliefs. She thinks that in order to exercise she should really enjoy it and not find it boring. She thinks that she cannot resist chocolate. She has angry thoughts and thinks that life is unfair. She tends to pity herself. She judges herself rather than judging her behaviour and attitude. She judges herself in an unhealthy way by seeing herself as a failure because she has failed to lose weight.

The result of such short-term comfort-seeking beliefs is that she is overweight and gripped in this self-fulfilling prophecy.

Lucy's unhealthy first belief about discomfort

Belief 1 – *I must have what I fancy (chocolate) whenever I want. I can't tolerate not having what I fancy when I want.*

Work out Lucy's Belief 2 and Belief 3 from the diagram below:

A	B	C
Trigger	Belief	Consequence
Seeing chocolate	B1	Emotion: Anxiety Behaviour: Eats chocolate Thought: I can't stop myself Symptom: Overweight
Not feeling instant enjoyment when exercising	B2	Emotion: Anxiety Behaviour: Gives up Thought: I'm not enjoying this so what's the point? Symptom: Overweight
Boredom	B3	Emotion: Anxiety Behaviour: Gives up Thought: I'll talk to someone instead of exercising Symptom: Overweight

Lucy's unhealthy beliefs about life
Emotion – anger and frustration with life

Belief 1 – *It's so unfair that other people manage to lose weight. I must lose weight easily like the people I read about. Life is not fair and it should be fair. I can't stand that life is unfair.*

The following is the ABC chain for the above belief.

A	B	C
Trigger	Belief	Consequence
Seeing a picture of skinny celebrity in magazine	B1	Emotion: Anger Behaviour: Sulk and throw magazine on the floor and go and eat instead Thought: It's so unfair. Life is bad Symptom: Overweight

Lucy's unhealthy beliefs about her failure to lose weight
Emotion – depression

Belief 1 – *I have failed at losing weight and I should succeed at losing weight. Failing proves I'm a failure.*

The following is the ABC chain for the above belief.

A	B	C
Trigger	Belief	Consequence
Noticing the fact she's overweight	B1	Emotion: Depression Behaviour: Eat more and abstain from going to the gym Thought: I'm ugly and useless Symptom: Overweight

Identify why the beliefs are unhealthy

Are they consistent or inconsistent with reality? Why?

Do they make sense? Are they logical or illogical? Why?

Are they helpful or unhelpful? Do they help or hinder her? Why?

Changing her beliefs requires a change in understanding. Lucy has to understand that in order to lose weight she has to stay focused on her goal and not give in to instant gratification. She has to understand that she can learn to enjoy exercising even though in the short term it will feel boring and not very enjoyable. She has to understand that in order to lose weight she has to give up her short-term, comfort-seeking beliefs and adopt an attitude of long-term gain, that is no pain, no gain (or no weight loss). Once Lucy has understood the healthy solution to her problem, she will need to think in accordance with the healthy versions of her current beliefs, and start taking action that fits with those beliefs. In essence, Lucy will start applying what she now understands.

LONG-TERM GAIN

It is easy to understand why you want to strive to fulfil your dreams and goals. As children we daydream about how we want the future to be. Maybe you saw yourself as a sports star, a doctor, or married with your own children. As you grow up you start striving for those future ambitions and imagine yourself enjoying that achievement and the rewards it brings.

As an adult, pursuing long-term goals can become the sole focus. You may find yourself always working towards something. Working towards goals can become a way of living, and work begins to dominate your life in an unhealthy way.

When you work towards your long-term goals at the expense of all other important parts of your life, problems can arise. You can experience emotional problems like anxiety, depression and lack of joy, and health problems caused by eating the wrong things, drinking too much or lack of exercise. There may also be family, relationship or friendship issues. If you know that your long-term focus is finite and that you will introduce a balance in your life, provided your family and friends are supportive you may not experience any problems. However, if you are experiencing problems because you are focused on long-terms goals at the expense of other important things in your life, it may be appropriate to reflect on your strategy and evaluate it.

When you work in accordance with your long-term strategies alone, you probably work late and at weekends and choose work commitments instead of social or family ones. If this approach is relentlessly maintained over a long period of time, you will feel comfortable when you are working and feel uncomfortable when you are relaxing, having fun and engaging in short-term leisure activities. You will find yourself thinking about work and what you have to do. Not only will you be stressed when you accept social invitations, but your friends will also feel the strain.

It is useful to reflect on whether you are focusing on your long-term goals in a dysfunctional way. You will know this is the case if your spouse, partner or friends have been complaining about it, or you may feel uncomfortable whenever you socialize, feeling that you should be working.

You may also feel anger and resentment towards the people who are close to you because you think they are putting too much pressure on you to spend more time with them.

BALANCE

In the previous two sections you were introduced to the notion of short-term comfort and long-term gain. You learned that if your beliefs are about a need for short-term comfort, fun and enjoyment, you will find it very difficult to achieve goals. The failure to achieve goals can then trigger other emotional problems. You will know how to have fun and do things that instantly gratify your desires, but you will be chasing this state of comfort as a priority. This in turn will lead you to give up on your long-term goals because long-term goals require you to commit to them, to put in effort and to work at them in a consistent manner.

You now understand that all work and no play can also lead to emotional and relationship problems. You can see that working towards the long term implies sacrificing other things. If you are happy to do that, it is your choice, but if this long-term gain focus is triggering emotional and relationship problems and you are not feeling happy, you may need to introduce a balance. In this case you will need to have some short-term comfort strategies.

The balance is about healthy short-term comfort strategies and healthy long-term gain focus. To bring this about you will need to reflect on the things that matter to you and bring them back into your awareness, by focusing and actively doing something about it. It requires you to change your currently held unhealthy beliefs into their healthy versions.

FALLIBILITY

As human beings, we are all fallible and imperfect. The results are that we will make mistakes, get things wrong, misunderstand, fail and experience disappointment and frustrations. Given this truth, how do you think we should respond to our fallibilities? You can, of course, get irrationally angry, anxious, frustrated, depressed and behave in accordance with your emotions. Does that help your search for happiness in either the short or long term? In reality it results in misery and unhappiness, and you end up tackling things in a way that limits what you can achieve. In many instances it causes you to sabotage the things you want and desire.

Accepting your human imperfection frees you to think in a constructive and positive way. It enables you to be goal-directed, opening you up to learn and find creative solutions when you do mess things up. Acceptance of fallibility is the opposite to being stuck. It does not mean that by accepting your imperfection you somehow excuse it and justify inaction. As long as your goal is significant to you, you learn to do things better and develop a healthy attitude to it.

I was told a story about a hardworking schoolgirl who was a high achiever. Her teachers noticed that her grades were getting worse. She was getting very worried about making mistakes, to such an extent that she began to make more mistakes. Her confidence in her own abilities was diminishing. After some time her teachers decided to mention this to her parents. Her parents did not want to put pressure on her by telling her, and decided to demonstrate how making mistakes is not the end of the world. They wanted to show her that when people make mistakes they can respond in a different way by accepting it, expressing disappointment, thinking about what they could learn and how to move on. They wanted to prove that she could learn from her mistakes without putting herself down and not view making mistakes as a catastrophe. Without telling her what they were going to do, they planned a whole weekend of making mistakes. They pretended to receive news about failures, then dealt with it all in a healthy and positive way, expressing feelings of disappointment and talking about what to do about it. They also involved her in some of the things they had planned and made sure that she witnessed them making mistakes. After that weekend, her teachers reported a change in her attitude. She was not anxious, instead showing healthy frustration and disappointment, coming up with solutions and talking about what she would do next time a similar thing happened.

SUMMARY

Goal achievement depends mainly on your attitude. According to CBT, healthy and rational beliefs enable you to achieve your goals and unhealthy, irrational beliefs sabotage them. In essence, if you are not achieving your goals, and are feeling unhealthy negative emotions like anxiety and depression, your current reality is supported by unhealthy beliefs that are keeping you stuck in this state. Your goal, which is the vision you have about how you want to be and what you want to achieve, needs to be supported by a different set of beliefs – the healthy or rational beliefs that provoke you to experience well-being and enable your success.

I, you, the world

The beliefs you hold can be split into three areas: I, you, and the world. You can have unhealthy beliefs about yourself, another person or about the world or life in general. Alternatively, you can hold healthy beliefs about yourself, another person or the world. It is useful to remember that no one has purely unhealthy or healthy beliefs. We all have a mixture of both, so we may have unhealthy beliefs about work but healthy ones about friendships.

When you think about unhealthy and healthy beliefs you can understand that emotional disturbance is largely caused by unhealthy beliefs. There are potentially 12 types of belief as the following table illustrates:

	Must	Awful	Unbearable	Worthless
I	*I must have xyz*	*If I don't have xyz it's awful*	*If I don't have xyz it's unbearable*	*If I don't have xyz I am worthless*
You	*You must xyz*	*It's awful if you don't*	*It's unbearable if you don't*	*You are worthless*
The world	*The world must xyz*	*It's awful when it doesn't*	*It's unbearable when it doesn't*	*The world is worthless*

Healthy beliefs are finite. They balance the unhealthy concepts above by bringing reality to them, as illustrated below:

	Prefer but accept that it might not be	Bad but not awful	Difficult but bearable	Imperfect but worthwhile
I	*I prefer to have xyz but I accept that I might not*	*If I don't have xyz it would be bad but not awful*	*If I don't have xyz it would be difficult but bearable*	*If I don't have xyz I am fallible but worthy*

You	It would be good if you did xyz but you don't have to	It's bad but not awful if you don't	It's difficult but bearable if you don't	You are fallible but worthy
The world	It would be good if the world was xyz but I accept that sometimes it isn't	It's bad but not awful when it isn't	It's difficult but bearable when it isn't	The world is imperfect but worthwhile

Understanding

Changing beliefs requires you to understand that they trigger feelings, thoughts, behaviours and symptoms. First you need to understand what your unhealthy beliefs provoke you to think, do and feel, and then what their healthy versions would result in.

Apply what you understand

The next step is to apply your understanding consistently, even daily, with energy and a sense of forcefulness. You need to stop thinking and acting in accordance with your unhealthy beliefs in the here and now and start thinking and behaving in accordance with your healthy beliefs. This is when you will feel tension and discomfort but, as you know, this is necessary because you are changing old and unhealthy thinking and behavioural habits. You cannot make long-lasting change if you understand what needs to be done and don't do it because it feels difficult.

Tolerating tension

The tension you experience can be tolerated more easily if you focus on your goal and the personal benefits it brings.

The reasons that remind you of why you are making this change are called the 'what's in it for me' reasons. Your goal and your 'what's in it for me' reasons should be at the forefront of your mind so you think and remind yourself of them daily to keep you motivated.

Momentum

Maintaining the process of change in a consistent way is key. It is important that you keep the momentum going. This requires thinking differently, doing things differently, repeating and keeping going until you arrive at your goal or until your feelings change. Imagine, for example, that you are driving a steam train. You need to keep putting enough coal in to keep it going towards its destination. It will help you to keep going if you see your work on your healthy beliefs in that way, so that you understand that you will need to keep at it until you arrive at where you want to be in terms of emotional change.

It is likely that you will face obstacles along the way as you are pursuing your goals. It is important that you do not take your eye off your goal but find a way around each obstacle in turn. As you make progress, the kinds of obstacle you deal with will change. As you become more successful, you will have different kinds of problems from the ones that arose when you started. For example, at one time you were worried about how to develop your business, now you are worried about the conflict you are having with your suppliers. Viewing the latter problem as a sign of progress will remind you that you have moved on from the past.

Accepting fallibility

Lastly, remember that you are fallible and this means you will experience failure and disappointment. The attitude you take to these likely eventualities is what will keep you healthy and happy in the long term.

Summary of the CBT process of change and goal accomplishment

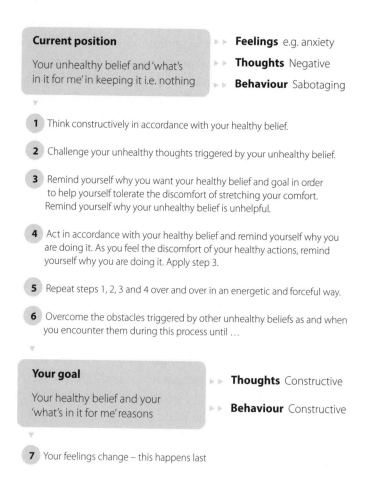

Current position

Your unhealthy belief and 'what's in it for me' in keeping it i.e. nothing

▸ ▸ **Feelings** e.g. anxiety

▸ ▸ **Thoughts** Negative

▸ ▸ **Behaviour** Sabotaging

1 Think constructively in accordance with your healthy belief.

2 Challenge your unhealthy thoughts triggered by your unhealthy belief.

3 Remind yourself why you want your healthy belief and goal in order to help yourself tolerate the discomfort of stretching your comfort. Remind yourself why your unhealthy belief is unhelpful.

4 Act in accordance with your healthy belief and remind yourself why you are doing it. As you feel the discomfort of your healthy actions, remind yourself why you are doing it. Apply step 3.

5 Repeat steps 1, 2, 3 and 4 over and over in an energetic and forceful way.

6 Overcome the obstacles triggered by other unhealthy beliefs as and when you encounter them during this process until …

Your goal

Your healthy belief and your 'what's in it for me' reasons

▸ ▸ **Thoughts** Constructive

▸ ▸ **Behaviour** Constructive

7 Your feelings change – this happens last

This book has provided you with the information and constructive tools to help you work in accordance with the laws of nature and in a way that is consistent with reality. The aim is to help you strive for excellence and long-term happiness.

Be mindful of lapsing into the old but familiar habits of thinking and behaving. A lapse is a minor occurrence and is very common. Two steps forward, and occasionally one step back. Use the concepts in this book to deal with minor lapses. This ensures continued progress. If, however, you do not deal with minor lapses as and when they occur, you will be at risk of a relapse. A relapse is a significant return to the state you were in when you experienced your problem. You can of course deal with a relapse in the same way, but it is far easier to deal with minor lapses.

About the Author

Avy Joseph is an experienced Cognitive Behaviour Therapist, lecturer and Director and Co-founder of the companies College of Cognitive Behavioural Therapies and City Minds. He is a registered and accredited therapist with the British Association for Behavioural and Cognitive Psychotherapies (BABCP) and The Association of Rational Emotive Behaviour Therapists (AREBT). He has published *Confidence and Success with CBT* and *Visual CBT* with Maggie Chapman, Co-founder of the College.

Index

Index

Index

Index

Index